Napoleon

Napoleon

Keith Addey

Series Editors
Michael and Mollie Hardwick

Evergreen Lives

ISBN 0 7127 0005 6

Series Editors
Michael and Mollie Hardwick

Design by Roy Lee

Production by Bob Towell

Colour Separations
by
D.S. Colour International Limited, London
Photo-typesetting
by
Sayers Clark Limited, Croydon, Surrey

Printed and bound in Spain by
TONSA, San Sebastian

Contents

Select Bibliography

CORRELLI BARNETT - *Bonaparte* (London 1978).

DAVID G. CHANDLER - *The Campaigns of Napoleon* (New York 1966).

DAVID G. CHANDLER - *Dictionary of The Napoleonic Wars* (London 1979).

PIETER GEYL (Trans. from Dutch by Olive Renier) - *Napoleon: For and Against* (reissue, Penguin 1965).

MICHAEL GLOVER - *The Napoleonic Wars: an Illustrated History* (London 1979).

J.E. HOWARD - *Letters and Documents of Napoleon* (London 1961).

DAVID STACTON - *The Bonapartes* (New York 1966).

J.M. THOMPSON - *Napoleon Bonaparte: His Rise and Fall* (Oxford 1952).

Chronology

1769 Birth of Napoleon (then Napoleone Buonaparte) at Ajaccio, Corsica, 15 August.

1778 Enters Military School at Brienne in France, remaining until October 1784.

1784 Gains entry to the *École Militaire*, Paris.

1785 His father dies. Napoleon graduates and takes up his commission in the artillery in September.

1789 The French Revolution. Fall of the Bastille, 14 July.

1791 Napoleon returns to Corsica. Takes part in local political upheaval.

1793 Returns to Paris. Execution of Louis XVI on 21 January. France declares war on Britain in February. Assassination of Marat in July. Napoleon distinguishes himself at siege of Toulon, December.

1796 Marries Josephine de Beauharnais on 9 March and leaves to command French Army of Italy.

1797 End of the victorious Italian campaign.

Napoleon returns in triumph to Paris and enforces martial law.

1798 Appointed C-in-C Army of the Orient and invades Egypt. French army stranded there by defeat in naval Battle of the Nile.

1799 Napoleon defeats British and Turks on land at Aboukir in July. Returns to France and becomes one of Consulate of Three, replacing The Directory.

1800 Napoleon made First Consul in February. Leads an army across the Alps in May to fight the Austrians. Battle of Marengo, 14 June.

1801 Britain invades and liberates Egypt.

1802 Napoleon made First Consul for life. Peace with England under Treaty of Amiens, 25 March.

1803 War resumed, 17 May.

1804 Napoleon crowned Emperor on 2 December.

1805 Plan to invade England foiled by Nelson's destruction of Franco-Spanish fleet at Trafalgar, 21 October. Napoleon defeats Austro-Russian armies at Austerlitz, 2 December.

1806 Defeats Prussians at Battle of Jena in October and enters Berlin.

1807 Defeats Russians at Eylau in February. Falls in love with Countess Marie Walewska at Warsaw. Meets Tsar Alexander I at Tilsit planning alliance to defeat Britain.

1808 Invades Spain, appoints his brother Joseph its King.

1809 British driven out of Spain. Defeat of Austrians

at Wagram in July, ending Franco-Austrian war in Treaty of Schönbrunn, 14 October. Napoleon divorces Josephine in December.

1810   Marries Archduchess Marie Louise of Austria, April.

1811   Birth of Napoleon's heir, Francois Charles Joseph (*l'Aiglon*), in March. He is created King of Rome.

1812   Napoleon invades Russia. Battle of Borodino, September, and entry into Moscow. Retreat from Russia begins in October.

1813   Coalition of Allies leads to defeat of Napoleon at Leipzig in 'Battle of the Nations', October. Wellington drives French from Spain and invades France.

1814   Napoleon abdicates, 11 April. Exiled to Elba, arriving 4 May. Louis XVIII returns as King of France. Congress of Vienna convened.

1815   Napoleon escapes from Elba and lands in France on 1 March. Finally defeated at Waterloo, 18 June. Abdicates again and attempts to escape to America. Surrenders to Royal Navy, 15 July. Exiled to St Helena, arriving in October.

1821   Death of Napoleon on 5 May.

Introduction

THE NAME OF NAPOLEON BONAPARTE has become, in the country he hated and sought to destroy, almost an element of the language: 'A Napoleon of crime', 'a Napoleon of commerce' are titles automatically given to men who have risen to the top of their chosen ladders; some of whom, indeed, have consciously modelled themselves on him. The image is one of determination and dominance, grandeur, spectacular achievement, heroism and patriotism. It is salutary to note that many of those who have assumed it have also been ruthless, despotic, megalomanic and mother-dominated. A study of Napoleon's own life reveals the presence in it of every one of these qualities and defects. 'A regular little Napoleon' implies a petulant, self-important bully, who has set himself above his rightful station. He was that, too; but an entire nation sustained him in his estimate of himself, with its love and its blood.

The man who is France's supreme hero was not a Frenchman, but a Corsican, whose father was engaged in guerrilla warfare against the French. The boy grew up hating the French, a hatred not diminished by the attitude of his fellow-pupils at the *École Militaire* where he appeared as a rough, uncouth, surly lad hardly able to speak or understand the French language. His patriotism seems not to have been deep, since when it suited his ambition to do so he almost casually abandoned the cause of

Corsican freedom and attached himself to the ideals of Revolutionary France.

Not that he was even a natural revolutionary, a son of the people: the Buonapartes were of decent if rather obscure lineage, with a number of soldiers on the family tree. His identification with the Revolution came about because he happened to be on the spot when the chaos in France that followed The Terror gave him the perfect opportunity to assert a natural capacity for leadership. France, close to civil war, torn apart between royalists and Girondins, was the nursery of his fame. Cold, calculating, apolitical, self-centred, he saw before him a very tall ladder, with its lower rungs invitingly unoccupied, and did not hesitate to set his feet on them.

He climbed up rapidly. Made a brigadier at twenty-four, after capturing Toulon from British hands, by twenty-six he was Commander of the Army of the Interior and a major-general. A year later he was Commander of the Army of Italy, victor in twenty-six battles spread over less than a year, overrunning widespread territories and able to send home to bankrupt France immense quantities of loot - money, pictures and manuscripts. By the age of thirty he had added political ascendancy to military eminence and become First Consul, supreme authority in France.

At thirty-four he crowned himself Emperor, and prepared to found a dynasty, bestowing crowns on his brothers and organising his sisters into advantageous marriages. The 'revolutionary' had become a king-maker, the old ways of the banished Bourbons had returned, an Imperial nobility making the Revolution seem a mere dream. And in Vienna, Ludwig van Beethoven, whose music spoke for all men in chains, tore out the dedication he had intended for Napoleon in his *Eroica* Symphony, declaring, 'Now he will trample underfoot all the Rights of Man and only indulge his ambition: he will set himself on high, like all the others, and become a tyrant!'

As Beethoven's gesture implied, true heroism requires some degree of nobility of character, of chivalry and compassion, of humility in triumph, and they are qualities which Napoleon seems conspicuously to have lacked. Human life was of little account to him; by his own admission he cared nothing for the lives of a million men, and he commented on the 'beauty' of the battlefield of Borodino, strewn with its 80,000 slain. He was perfectly ready to massacre anyone who menaced or even resented him.

In personal relationships the same ruthlessness characterised him. He loaded his family with honours, but ruled them and their private lives with all the rigour of a Corsican patriarch. He and his wife Josephine are often included in catalogues of the world's greatest lovers, but after his early display of violent Italianate passion towards her his attitude seems to have been that of a merely dutiful husband, not so devoted that he made any attempt to remain faithful to her. Women in general were to him either objects of lust or 'wombs' for the production of the heir who should found the Bonaparte dynasty. A less romantic man, in the popular sense, never existed. Godless, loveless and friendless, he lived for himself and the power he worshipped.

To admire Napoleon, then, it is necessary to turn to his achievements. He was a brilliant and tireless campaigner, one whose mental vision could take in the annexation of countries and continents as easily as another leader might have planned the next step of a battle. Through his genius France became the ruler of Europe. Yet this was not the doing of genius alone. If Fame is the spur, Luck is the mount on which men of destiny ride into immortality; and luck of the most amazing kind was Napoleon's from the time when he found himself in France when she most needed an inspired leader. Time and again his luck saved him from defeat and death, turned the tide of battle in his favour, directed him upwards. When luck failed him, it was because of his ultimately fatal weakness, the impatience which drove him to embark on an extreme course of action without taking into account insuperable obstacles.

He wanted the East, but forgot to include in his

calculations the geography of Egypt. He looked on Britain as a contemptible foe, easy of conquest, but overlooked the strength and professionalism of the Royal Navy. He set his sights on Russia: 'I go to Moscow not from fancy or self-gratification, but out of dry calculation.' The dry calculation omitted to note the distance between Russia and France, the inevitable coming of the terrible Russian winter, and the fact that troops and horses need regular supplies of provisions.

His luck left him, deservedly, and he crawled back, beaten, his *Grande Armée* reduced to a straggle, tens of thousands of frozen corpses marking the way he had come from burning Moscow. But never mind; he was able to assure an anxious Europe that 'His Majesty's health has never been better.'

The peoples whose lands he overran hated him, so he put them to the sword. The French, however, went on loving him, and there were always fresh armies ready to die for him, as a great many of them did. France has good reason for her continued adulation of him. He ruled her more positively than she had ever been ruled before. He reformed her administration and pulled together her chaotic legal system, giving her the *Code Napoleon* which evolved into the *Code Civil*, the basis of most modern European civil law. Perhaps more importantly, he gave France a figure of romance such as she had not had since Charlemagne. He was the giant-killer who became a giant, the Little Man who called himself, in the name of France, 'God of Fortune and of War'.

The English poet Cowper saw him as the 'Chief monster that has plagued the nations yet', and the twentieth-century historian A.J.P. Taylor has echoed him:

> He was a monster. He found France great; he left her small... It would have been better for everyone if he had never been born.

A monster he was, perhaps; but to France a *monstre sacré*. Fifty years and more after his death French children begged for their favourite bedtime story:

'Parlez-nous de lui, grand'mère -parlez-nous de lui.'

He would like to be remembered by them, for he loved children, and they him; and an English child on St Helena was to be one of his last friends.

Michael and Mollie Hardwick

Good Material

1769 – 1785

ONE AUGUST DAY in the year 1769 a nineteen-year-old girl walked slowly down a street of Ajaccio, the capital of Corsica. She was heavily pregnant, so that walking was difficult, but it was the day of the Feast of the Assumption of the Blessed Virgin, and she was determined to attend Mass in the Cathedral church.

Suddenly, almost at the church door, she knew she dare go no farther. She turned and hurried back as best she could to the tall house she had left a few minutes before. It was all she could do to get upstairs before her labour was over as suddenly as it had come on. There was no time to get to a bed; very unceremoniously Napoleone Buonaparte arrived on the parlour floor.

The floor was cold and hard, no doubt, and he protested very loudly for such a puny, undersized baby. Long years afterwards he was to tell a doctor that the room had been carpeted richly, the fabric woven with heroic figures - Caesar, Alexander, and others. It was a typical flight of fancy by one for whom nothing, in his own view, could be too good.

The baby born on 15 August, appropriately under the dominant sign of Leo, was lucky to have been born alive. Only a few weeks before his birth his father and mother had been journeying dangerously. Carlo-Maria Buonaparte had been one of the leaders under the patriot hero General Pascal Paoli in Corsica's war of independence against her conqueror,

France. In the journey through rough wild country they came to the river Liamone, its waters running high. Letizia's horse missed its footing, and was carried away down the river, while her husband shouted to her to let go and swim for her life. But with grim determination she hung on and brought the horse and herself safely to the bank.

An irony which would not be appreciated until historians looked back at the circumstances of this child's birth was that, instead of setting out on the perilous journey home, the young Buonapartes, with their eldest son, eighteen-month-old Joseph, and the unborn baby might have been on their way to England. The defeated General Paoli had taken refuge there, and Carlo-Maria had wanted to follow him. But Letizia's condition was too far advanced, so he changed his mind. A little persuasion from her, or some other circumstance, and the great enemy of England might have been born an Englishman.

Carlo-Maria Buonaparte was not by nature a soldier, but a gentle man with literary tastes. He came of reasonably good family, owning the 'four quarters of nobility', some land with vineyards and olive trees and two houses. The family was by no means poor, yet not well-off, so that when Napoleon's social status came to be questioned after the Revolution he was easily able to disclaim the stigma of being an aristocrat, of which he had not been ashamed to boast before. Letizia was proud, handsome, intelligent - and illiterate. She eventually learned to read and write, but never really mastered French or smoothed out her Corsican accent. Good material for a hero's mother, she always preserved an attitude of cool realism towards the meteoric rise of the extraordinary duckling she had hatched among her brood of thirteen.

Eight of them survived, five boys and three girls. In 1784, Carlo-Maria began to fail in health, and in February 1785 he died, aged almost thirty-nine, probably from cancer. Letizia, left to bring up her family alone, loved all her children and dealt fairly with them, including the unattractive Napoleone, who was aggressive and self-centred, 'a quarreller, full of mischief', as he later admitted himself, given

to bullying and lying: an uncle prophesied a spectacular future for him because of his facility in telling fibs. He had a gift for throwing tantrums, some
real, some assumed in order to get his own way.

He had intelligence, however; a bent for mathematics and a gift for military games. His brother
Joseph remembered, ruefully, how Napoleone
would always get the best place and the biggest
slice of everything. At school, when the children
had been divided into two sections and positioned
under two large flags, the Carthaginian and the
Roman, Napoleone flew into a furious temper at
finding himself under the Carthaginian, while
Joseph was a Roman. They eventually changed
places, of course; class-room discipline did not ex-
ist for Joseph's younger brother.

When he turned nine his life changed abruptly.
Two years earlier his father had put his name down
for one of the French *Écoles Militaires*. For the first
time the boys, aged eleven and nine, left their
sunny island off the west coast of Italy. A sea voyage brought them to Marseilles, then they travelled
overland northwards to Autun, in Burgundy.

The France they came to in this year of 1778 was
as yet unshaken by revolution, but the elements of
it were present. The Throne and the Government
seemed in no danger of attack, but reforms were
needed. Voltaire, leader of the '*Philosophes*', working from his estate close to the Swiss border, where
he had launched many domestic reforms of his own,
had set out in his great novel *Candide* the necessity
for mankind to do its best to change itself for the
better. His battle-cry (sometimes used instead of
his signature on letters) was '*Écrasez l'Infâme!*' -
'Crush the Infamous!' The Infamous, to him, were
those who exercised intolerance and persecution,
bigotry, unfair privilege, believed in superstitions,
and pursued the empty folly of war. The power of
his pen helped to change public opinion. When, in
1778, he came home to Paris after nearly thirty
years, the crowds mobbed him, shouting their welcome. In the same year he died, not living to see the
violent, bloody working out of his ideals in a way he
had not imagined. Soon the weak King Louis XVI

would be forced into open conflict with the *parlements*, and both would be losers in the anarchy that was to come.

But when Napoleone arrived in France the military scene was reasonably bright. The successes of such French commanders as Lafayette and Rochambeau in the American war had revived a warlike spirit; military instruction was taken seriously, schools of artillery and engineering had been founded; the royal army was in its last distinguished days.

It was early January and bitterly cold. Nobody understood what the brothers said, for they spoke with the rough dialect of Corsica, very different from classical Italian, and they were quite unused to French. But the Abbé Chardon was a determined and firm teacher. After four months, by which time Napoleone had a fair grasp of French (though he was never to speak it perfectly), the brothers were parted, Joseph 'all in tears', Napoleone restraining any emotion he might have felt, other than a single tear.

The *École Militaire* of Brienne, in Champagne, barely a day's ride from Paris, was hardly a more friendly place for Napoleone than Autun had been. It was run by monks, the Minimes of the Order of St Benedict; although it purported to give a military education, it did little more than teach the usual school subjects to the sons of gentlemen, and preach religion, with a course in fortification thrown in during the last year. The discipline was more suited to anchorites than growing boys: only one blanket on the bed of the cubicle (locked at night, no midnight larks), prayer and study all day from 6 a.m. to 8 p.m. When Letizia came to see her son she was worried at his thinness.

The French boys despised Napoleone. He, still fiercely Corsican, reacted with retaliatory hatred, bursts of violence, and gloom. He took refuge in solitude and study. Though not in any sense intellectual, he was very good at mathematics and history. Theology he despised, and from this time came his life-long hatred of religion. The ignorant, innocent monks of Brienne were unknowingly preparing trouble for their Church, even for their Pope.

Napoleone had been destined for the navy, but sometime during these years he decided that he would prefer the artillery. Aged fifteen, he left the school at Brienne on 30 October 1784 without many regrets on either side and joined the *École Militaire* in Paris, taking up a free place as a gentleman cadet, awarded by King Louis XVI for his achievements in mathematics. He was now where he surely wished to be, in an establishment run like an army without the inconvenience of war, but with drum-beats and smart uniforms, a fine classical building fronting on the *Champ de Mars*, no more monks, no more austerity. Yet he was still a solitary, still suspicious of people, conscious of his own social inferiority among these haughty young Frenchmen, hating them for their very Frenchness, to the point of earning rebuke from the staff; he was politely told to moderate his love for Corsica.

After a year there he passed the entrance examination for places in artillery schools comfortably enough, if not brilliantly, coming forty-second out of fifty-eight, and received his commission with the rank of 2nd lieutenant. He was the only Corsican to have qualified from the school, and very proud of it. Splendid in a uniform of blue and scarlet, which made the best of his short stature, he proceeded to his chosen regiment, *La Fére-Artillerie*, at Valence, in the Dauphiné.

On the way, he and his young friend Alexandre Demazis paused to dine at Fontainebleau. If Napoleon (for so he now called himself) had been of a psychical nature, what shadows of the future might have passed before him at that table.

'I Quit Corsica'

1785 – 1793

VALENCE WAS A PLEASANT town of the Midi, probably homely to one brought up in small Ajaccio. Napoleon, after reporting to his regimental commander, went to his lodgings at the house of Monsieur Bou, a leading townsman with a comfortable home, luxurious after Spartan quarters in Paris. The unmarried daughter of the house, Mademoiselle Marie-Claudine Bou, though fifty years old, was no soured spinster, but kindly and maternal. For the first time Napoleon found himself treated tenderly by a woman: his mother loved him deeply, but he had felt the weight of her hand frequently. His youth - he was only sixteen - attracted Mlle Bou more than his appearance: he is described at this time as thin, narrow-shouldered, pale and hollow-cheeked, with long lank hair, a low voice, and an expression which might be taken for firmness, or, less charitably, irritability.

He was shy, still burdened with deep inferiority. But gradually he began to make friends through the influence of the amiable Bous. Madame Gregoire du Colombier was one of them. Charming, intelligent, a little older than Mille Bou, she took the awkward boy under her wing, making him realise that the company of a middle-aged woman could be highly rewarding in a perfectly chaste way. For her daughter Caroline, a little older than himself, his feelings were more conventionally romantic. She did not take his courting at all seriously, but he reminisced about her towards the end of his life in most affectionate terms, and showed his enduring feelings by rewarding her husband with a barony. He seems to have been a timid suitor, already displaying the gaucherie in dealings with women which never left him.

Happier than when he had come to Valence, he set out in early September 1786 for Corsica on leave. He had been away from home for seven years and nine months. The family were assembled to give him a hero's welcome, this dashing young officer who had left them as a little boy of nine. But his father had died the previous year, and there were serious money troubles. The nursery of mulberry trees which Carlo-Maria had begun with the Government's permission had been abandoned when the Government changed its mind. The income Letizia had relied on from them was not forthcoming. Archdeacon Lucien Buonaparte, Carlo-Maria's brother, had acted as a second father to the family, but he was elderly now and ailing.

Napoleon acted with characteristic impetuosity. He requested an extension of his leave, with pay, and took himself to Paris. Whether the action he took there was singularly clever, or whether the authorities were dazed by the sheer cheek of this very young man, he gained the entrée to the highest circles. It did not settle the affair of the missing mulberry trees and his mother's finances, but it gave him confidence and important contacts. He also applied himself to lighter things, such as the theatre and women. One winter evening, strolling in the alleys of the Palais Royal, noted for the disreputables who haunted them, he encountered a very young woman whose timid air encouraged him to speak to her (though in his later written account he priggishly noted his repugnance to her class). His curiously prim questions - 'Is there nothing healthier you could do for a living? Do you regret your fall?' - ended in his taking her back to the Hôtel de Cherbourg, in the rue du Faubourg St Honoré. He called this in his Memoirs a 'Philosophical Experience'.

Before returning to his regiment in June 1788 he

spent more time in Corsica, still deeply troubled by his mother's poverty. It irked him that in spite of the fine official connections he had made in Paris he had been unable to help her. Joseph was away at Pisa, so she had no man of the family at her side. Memories of this grim period made the honours he heaped upon 'Madame Mère' in later years all the more satisfying to him.

The regiment was now stationed at Auxonne in Burgundy. The small town was a quiet one, offering few temptations to do anything but study, which he badly needed to do after so long an absence on his own affairs. For fifteen months he worked intensively, going to bed at ten and getting up at four. Mathematics, with its dependence on logic, appealed to him greatly; he was never tired of making calculations, compiling digests of historical facts (including a history of England up to the expulsion of James II), listing information drawn from geography, religion, classical literature, and making himself a theoretical master of military tactics and procedure. His abnormally large head might have been designed for filling with facts, useful and useless. He was mentally omnivorous and responded willingly to the personal interest taken in him by the commandant, the veteran artillery officer General Jean Pierre du Teil.

Yet for much of his time at Auxonne he was ill, suffering from a fever and its effects, which may have come from the marshy lands bordering the river Sâone. His condition cannot have been helped by his eating habits; he believed that great merit lay in under-eating, taking only one meal a day, then going on to a milk diet, prescribed by himself. Throughout his life sensual pleasures seem to have been of very little concern to him, and any interest he might have taken in food and drink was offset by the lifelong hypochondria which began at an early age. Very real ills did sometimes attack him, but he had greater basic strength than he would ever admit.

In the notebooks he kept at Auxonne there are things reflecting another side of his character. A fascination with heroism, poetic and dramatic, appears in them, and a violent if undiscriminating admiration for the works and principles of Jean-Jacques Rousseau. Rousseau, the French-Swiss novelist and philosopher, had in 1762 produced *Le Contrat Social*, a discussion of the principles of political right, maintaining that the rightful authority is the general will, the will of the people, in fact. It began 'Man is born free; and everywhere he is in chains!' He proceeded to explain this by returning to the origins of human society, in which a 'social contract' was drawn up by early Man, individuals combining to group themselves 'under the supreme direction of the general will'. It was not a very well-informed conception, but it soon became a popular one to the many discontented with their lot, and to others seeking for some change in society. From this book came the motto of the French Revolution: *Liberté, Egalité, Fraternité.*

For all his feverishly intensive studies, Napoleon was not very adept at deducing rational theories from them. To him, tyrants could only be hereditary rulers, and dictatorships backed by the State could be only benevolent. He was to disprove this spectacularly from the beginning of his own Consulate. He accepted Rousseau's ideas without digesting them; the result for Europe would be an unhappy one.

In the notebooks, too, there are fragments of wildly romantic prose, also, perhaps, inspired by Rousseau's novel *La Nouvelle Héloïse*, and other popular expressions of what Madame de Staël called 'the burning agitations of the human heart'. Caroline de Colombier, far away in Valence, may have been still in his memory.

On 14 July 1789 there took place at Versailles that portentous exchange between King Louis XVI and the Duc de La Rochefoucauld-Liancourt, who had just brought him the news of the fall of the Bastille to the Parisian mob: 'Why, this is a revolt!' 'No, Sire, it is a revolution.'

The news took five days to reach Auxonne and spark off a corresponding outburst of long pent-up resentment against hunger, unemployment, high-handed officialdom and the aloof aristocracy. The rioting populace were soon joined by the troops who should have been restoring them to order. The staunch old commander, who four years later would be executed for his part in an uprising against the Paris Revolutionary régime, was left powerless, despite the support of a few officers.

Lt Buonaparte was not one of these. General du Teil had helped and considerably influenced him, but loyalty neither to him nor to the army could over-ride Napoleon's sympathy for the common people's cause against the Crown and the ruling classes. He had his career to think of, though, and his ambition resided in the army, so he compromised all round by applying for leave and hastening home to Corsica. It enabled him to keep his uniform and his rank, to distance himself from the ferment in mainland France, yet set himself up as a leader of the revolutionary movement in his native island. It was not his purpose to help Corsica's struggle to regain her independence; in fact, when the patriotic leader General Paoli returned from exile in London and soon began planning revolt against France, Napoleon and his family, who had been his supporters, turned their backs on him. Attaining prominence in his homeland seemed to Napoleon a useful preliminary to bidding for it in France as a whole.

Once more at this juncture his name might have become linked historically with Great Britain in a somewhat different way than was to be the case. Paoli, who would have liked him out of his way, advised him to go to England and get a commission in the British army, which he offered to help arrange for him. Napoleon declined: 'I preferred the French. I spoke their language, liked their manners, and thought the Revolution offered fine opportunities for an enterprising young man.' His aspirations were already extending beyond the military sphere. He became a founder member of the Ajaccio Jacobin (democratic) Club, wrote pamphlets propagating its ideals of absolute equality, and egged on his brother Joseph, now a local councillor, to use any means, including corruption and intimidation, to get the right people into key appointments.

Instead of becoming a British officer, Napoleon returned to his own regiment in France, completing his studies and unsuccessfully entering a competition with an essay on 'The Principles and Sentiments which should be inculcated into man in order to promote his Happiness.' According to it, ambition, leading to absolute power, was not to be recommended. When someone showed him the essay in later years he threw it on the fire, which by then was comment enough.

Considering the turbulence of the times, leave from the French army was easily obtained, and Napoleon was not backward in taking advantage of this. Vacationing was not his purpose, though; once more he hurried back to Corsica, to find out how he could make use of the unquiet situation there to advance his own position. One opening he had spotted was a new ruling that officers of lieutenant-colonel's rank and above were exempt from the general muster to arms due early next year. He had no hope of achieving any such rank by conventional promotion; but in Corsica, where the Buonapartes had influence and used it with Mafia-like ruthlessness, there was a volunteer force in which he would have no difficulty in getting senior rank. He had judged correctly, and, aged twenty-two, leaped effortlessly from lieutenant to lieutenant-colonel, second-in-command of a militia battalion.

Shrewd old General Paoli saw through that manoeuvre, recognising in the young officer a self-seeker, uninterested in the cause of Corsican independence. Having failed to get him from under his feet by persuading him to go to England, he revoked the raising of a further battalion whose command he had promised to Napoleon. This setback coincided with France's attempt to invade the Austrian Netherlands, at the end of April 1792, when a force of disgruntled regulars and inexperienced volunteers was put to flight by a handful of defenders and vented its frustration by shooting several of its own generals. Clearly, every available regular officer was needed back on duty to help mould a French army worthy of the name, and Lt Bonaparte's nominal colonelcy was not enough to exempt him.

The appearance of his name in the list of absentees whose appointments and pay had been discontinued was enough to send him scurrying back to Paris to seek reinstatement. He was lucky. His experience was regarded as more important than his indiscretion, and he was taken back on the strength, promoted to captain. It occurred to his younger brother Lucien that Napoleon was, to put it mildly, an opportunist, with the possibility of worse to come:

> I believe that he is a dangerous man; he seems to me to have the attributes of a tyrant, and I believe he would be one, if he were king, and that his name would become one of horror to posterity and to the sensitive patriot... No men are more detested in history that those who change with the wind; I perceive, and it is not only as of today, that in the event of a (further) revolution Napoleone would seek to keep himself at the top and even, for the sake of his material interests, I believe him to be capable of acting the turncoat.

That 'if he were king' reference suggests that such a notion had already been discussed between the brothers. King of Corsica, perhaps? It has the ring of something more substantial in the way of ambition than two young men exchanging daydreams. In Paris that August, Napoleon saw mob violence on the grand scale, when the Tuileries were stormed and disciplined regular soldiers were overwhelmed by sheer numbers and massacred. The following month, on 21 September, King Louis XVI was deposed and the Republic proclaimed, with a new calendar: 22 September was named 1 Vendemiaire, An. 1: in effect, time was beginning all over again. Whatever the mode of dating, the King had only four months of life left. His head, followed by Queen Marie-Antoinette's and those of countless other men and women of birth, breeding, achievement and culture, fell to the guillotine of 'The Terror' under which France now lived, and which sought to take its subjects' minds off tyranny and national bankruptcy by going to war with Europe. It was an excellent time to be an ambitious young career officer with a strong streak of remorselessness.

Corsica was as good as behind him now. He had gone back briefly, to escort his sister Marie-Anne, who was later to call herself Elisa, home from the convent school of St Cyr, which he thought no longer safe for her, and to take the political temperature of his homeland. He found nothing likely to bring him advantage, but did get his first experience of real military action, in February 1793, in charge of Corsican artillery supporting a French attack on the next-door island of La Maddalena. There was no early glory to be had, the assault ending in a scrambled evacuation, in which he had to suffer the ultimate humiliation of any artillery commander, abandoning his guns. But he had used them well, and confirmed the worth of training and discipline.

Politically, the Buonapartes' influence in Corsica was as good as over. Lucien Buonaparte had started moves to get General Paoli arrested as an enemy of the French Revolution. Too late, Napoleon, who foresaw the complications for his family and himself if a Corsican civil war should break out, with both sides hostile towards them, tried to head off this rash proposal, but failed. 'My presence was pointless; I quit Corsica,' he recorded later. 'Madame Mère' and the rest of them quit as well, to join forces again in France, at La Valette, near Toulon, from where they moved to Marseilles, the mother and five younger children settling into three humble rooms and an impoverished style of life.

To all intents and purposes it was the end of Napoleone Buonaparte's (he now used the French spelling of both names) association with the island of his birth. For his own purposes, he had identified himself with its fortunes to some degree, but left it without apparent regret or sentiment. The future was what mattered to him - *his* future. He was always on the lookout for his chances, and seized them when they came. Come they did, as coincidences of history served him well, guiding him along the way to becoming the very type of leader the French people thought they needed.

Into Immortality

1793 – 1796

NAPOLEON WORKED HARD at seeking out new advantages for himself, but he also possessed that faculty for recognising stray ones which happened to come along, and had the enterprise to seize them unhesitatingly and build on them for all that they were worth.

Not long after seeing his political aspirations dashed and his family wretchedly established in Toulon, he rode back to his regiment to get on with serving as a soldier of France. The French army at that time was an unwieldy mixture of well drilled soldiers of the deposed Bourbons and civilian volunteers, untrained and disobedient louts, eager to fight anyone and avid for pillage. In 1793 their country was at war with Prussia, Spain, the Netherlands, England and Italy, and the cry of '*La patrie en danger!*' was loud in the land as invasion of France seemed imminent. To add to this a pro-Bourbon uprising had developed in the south, where the citizens of the country's greatest naval arsenal, Toulon, had raised the Bourbon flag and welcomed ashore a combined force of British, Spanish and royalist *émigré* troops, under the supreme command of the British Admiral Lord Hood.

A French force commanded by General Jean François Carteaux, a sometime Court painter of little military experience, had laid siege to the port, but had no idea how to press it home. It was at this

33

time that Napoleon, on his way to the Italian front, chose to call on a fellow Corsican and former political colleague, Commissioner Antoine Christophe Saliceti, one of the civilian commissars with the army outside Toulon. The welcome he got was unexpectedly warm: 'Chance served us marvellously,' Saliceti exulted in his report to Paris. The artillery commander had been wounded and there was no one competent to replace him. Napoleon was ordered to take over forthwith.

He knew what to do, but how to do it was another matter. The available artillery was a mixture of types, with little ammunition for any of them, and scarcely anyone experienced in their use. General Carteaux and his staff were no help, smarting with damaged pride that an interloper should have been thrust on them as chief of artillery; but the overriding power lay in the civilian commissars' hands, and Napoleon went to work under their patronage.

It was his first battle, and he was faced with having to play the key role in overcoming a powerfully defended base with the British Mediterranean Fleet at anchor in its harbour. He was not to know that Admiral Hood was dissatisfied with the position and had little confidence in his heterogeneous force of 14,000, which included undisciplined Neapolitans, Sardinians and Spaniards, as well as British tars unused to serving as land soldiers. In theory, it amounted to a formidable defence, and plans were already afoot in Paris to organise a huge reinforcement of the 10,000 regulars and volunteers engaged in the siege. The young artillery officer had a much simpler plan: capture the two most commanding heights above the port, bring up every available gun, and threaten the fleet where it lay, with the likely result that it would up anchor and leave. He was opposed by General Carteaux, but supported by Citizen Saliceti. The attack was quickly launched. One of the heights was taken, but, due to Carteaux's halfhearted bungling, the defenders were left in possession of the more important one, Le Caire, on which they proceeded to build a formidable redoubt, Fort Mulgrave.

Realising that the siege had thereby been prolonged

indefinitely, Napoleon set to work discrediting Carteaux to the War Ministry. The commissars gave him their aid, and on 7 November the General departed, after handing over to an experienced veteran, General Jacques Dugommier, aged seventy-five. The tactics remained in Napoleon's hands, though, and he took his time over preparing the assault, a night attack on 17 December, in such unfavourable conditions that everything might have gone wrong. Old Dugommier, who had just been brought back out of retirement, could never have foreseen himself leading an assault in the early hours of a cold, wet morning against an impregnable-seeming strongpoint. He was wounded twice into the bargain, but determination won, and Fort Mulgrave was taken, Napoleon himself receiving his blooding in action with superficial wounds to the head and chest, and a British redcoat's bayonet thrust into his thigh, which seemed for a time likely to lose him the leg.

When daylight showed Lord Howe the enemy on the heights, positioning his guns in readiness to devastate his ships, he gave the order Napoleon had anticipated. The British warships crammed aboard as many sailors and soldiers as they could, and sailed with all haste. The abandoned French royalists held out briefly, to be massacred when the besieging force poured into Toulon on 19 December. On the order of the commissars, Napoleon Bonaparte was promoted immediately to brigadier. He would no longer need to contrive senior rank for himself; he had earned it. 'From that date,' wrote Comte Las Cases after Napoleon's death, 'history took him up, never to let him go. Then began his immortality.'

Meanwhile, in Marseilles, his older brother Joseph (b.1768) was furthering his fortune, and his hard-up family's, in less heroic fashion. Working as an aide to various People's Representatives, he had become acquainted with a wealthy soap merchant, Monsieur Clary, who had two daughters, one very pretty, the other very plain. It was the very plain one, Marie-Julie, who was of marriageable age, with a dowry of 150,000 francs. Joseph did not hesitate to make use of their friendship, and married her. What she lacked in looks, she made up for in goodness, and their happy marriage lasted fifty years.

It was the rising young officer brother who caught the fancy of the younger sister, Eugénie, a vivacious, sexy teenager. He responded by giving her the pet name Désirée, and they spent a good deal of time exchanging love-talk. It is unlikely that they went further, although Désirée at least would have been willing: she hid under his bed once, but almost certainly never got into it. After his marriage to Josephine, in 1796, Eugénie-Désirée took up with his friend and fellow republican Jean-Baptiste Bernadotte, who was thirty-five to her twenty-one when she married him in 1798. Bernadotte went on to become King of Sweden and Norway, and Joseph Bonaparte was made by his brother King of Naples and later King of Spain, so the soap-maker's daughters did quite well for themselves.

During this period of marrying, the unambitious one of the Bonaparte brothers, Lucien (b.1775), typically found a wife in his landlady's sister, Christine Boyer. For the other brother, Louis (b.1778), marriage came later, as it did for the three surviving girls, Elisa (b.1777), Pauline (b.1780), and Caroline (b.1782). As brothers and sisters of the man who was to dominate Europe, all the Bonapartes were translated from poverty to wealth and rank, though not invariably happiness. Only their mother, 'Madame Mère', insisted on a quiet life in a relatively unostentatious villa at Antibes, retaining the once-poor woman's apprehension that the glitter and prosperity were too good to last. When the collapse did come, her habitual caution and thrift helped soften the impact.

Although he had resisted the allures of Mlle Clary, Napoleon looked forward to marrying before too long. For the moment, though, he had matters of greater importance on hand. He had been appointed to command the artillery of the Army of Italy, giving him valuable experience of mountain warfare. At Toulon he had made the acquaintance of another rising political commissar,

Paul Barras (b.1755), while his old and helpful friend Saliceti had introduced him to the Robespierre brothers, Augustin and Maximilien, The Terror's hated leaders. Recognising the young officer's potential, Augustin Robespierre worked hard to advance his interest through the National Assembly, of which he was Secretary. It was, therefore, a blow to Napoleon to learn that discontent against The Terror had boiled over in revolt, and both Robespierres had been guillotined. The friendship he had cultivated with them was now an acute embarrassment: he was arrested and imprisoned while his associations with them and The Terror were investigated. Thanks to Saliceti again he was free within a fortnight and soon playing his other hand of cards by cultivating the late Robespierres' antagonist, Jean Barras, prominent in the new régime.

Circumstance proved obliging once more. In the autumn of 1795 it became obvious that another royalist uprising was imminent, this time in Paris. Barras, as Commander-in-Chief of the Army of the Interior, gave Napoleon command of the force detailed to break the revolt, which he proceeded to carry out with ruthless disregard for the fact that many of the mob which tried to storm the Tuileries, where the ruling Convention was in session on the 13th of Vendémiaire (5 October) were ordinary citizens protesting against continued repression, hardship and fear. Napoleon had long been contemptuous of mobs, whatever their cause, and he mowed this one down with grape-shot from cannon firing point-blank and withering musket fire. 'We killed plenty of them,' he told Joseph in a letter, adding, 'PS: Happiness is mine.'

He had cause to feel happy. He had crushed the rebellion in one day and been immediately promoted by the grateful Barras and his fellow Directors to take over his own role as C-in-C Army of the Interior, with particular responsibility for the Paris district. He was a full general, if an unlikely-looking one, according to a friend of the writer Stendhal who saw him:

He was the thinnest and oddest looking being I had met in my life. The dress of General Bonaparte would not have impressed anyone, and his appearance was so miserable that it was difficult at first for me to believe this man was a general.

Another eyewitness, the Duchesse d'Abrantes, observed him from a woman's view:

He was very careless of his personal appearance, and his long hair, which was badly combed and powdered, gave him a slovenly look... When I recollect Napoleon entering the courtyard of the Hotêl de la Tranquillité, with a shabby round hat drawn over his forehead, and his ill-powdered hair hanging over the collar of his grey greatcoat, without gloves, because he used to say they were a useless luxury, with boots ill-made and ill-polished, with his thinness and sallow complexion - when I recollect him at that time and think what he was afterwards I do not see the same man in the two pictures.

Unprepossessing and skinny though he may have been at that time, and certainly altogether unlike the well-known portrayals of the plump, scowling conqueror of Europe, he had no need to feel at a disadvantage. He had money and power and the highest connections; he was still only twenty-six, and every salon of the glitteringly raffish new Directoire set was open to him; and now he also had a woman he considered worth courting, Josephine de Beauharnais.

She was thirty-one, and a widow . She had been Marie-Josèphe Rose Tascher de la Pagerie, born in Martinique in the French West Indies, the daughter of a sugar-planter. At the age of sixteen she had been brought to Paris by her father to enter an arranged marriage with Alexandre, Vicomte de Beauharnais. Their union was a stormy one, but produced a son, Eugène (b. 1780) and a daughter, Hortense (b. 1783). At last, Alexandre's unfaithfulness proved more than Josephine could bear and she obtained a separation. In 1794 he was

arraigned as a traitor to the Revolution and guillotined a few days before Robespierre. Josephine
was also arrested and was to have suffered the same
fate, but the ending of The Terror on Robespierre's
death saved her and she was released.

She was free and widowed, but, as Mme Buonaparte had once been, desperately poor and with
children to maintain. She rented a house in Paris
and sent fourteen-year-old Eugène out as appren-
tice to a carpenter, and his eleven-year-old sister to
learn dressmaking. She herself managed to stay in
fashionable circulation, her eyes alert for a likely-
looking gentleman to offer her his protection. She
was appealingly pretty, judging from her numer-
ous portraits, with chestnut hair, a pert nose and a
sweet smile: someone referred to 'the seraphic
grace of her whole personality'.

The Barras household was one in which she was
welcome - more than welcome to Paul Barras himself, it had been rumoured, with the story that he at
length passed her on to Napoleon. They seem to
have met in October 1795; there is a romantic tale
that her brave little Eugène moved the Commander-in-Chief by stoutly calling on him to request
the return to his mother of their late father's hon-
oured sword. Napoleon consented, Josephine called on him to thank him, and they fell in love on the
instant. He wanted a woman to love, and she wanted
a man of means and position. Each wish was fulfilled.

It is questionable whether Josephine exactly
loved Napoleon, but, in his ardent, Italianate way,
he was infatuated with her:

> I awoke with my thoughts full of you. Your pic-
> ture and yesterday's intoxicating evening have
> given my senses no rest. Amazing indeed, sweet
> and incomparable Josephine, is the effect you
> have wrought within my heart... But there is
> more when, abandoning myself to that emotion
> which overcomes me utterly, I drink a flame of
> fire from your lips and from your heart!

In his St Helena days he maintained that he had
never really loved anyone else in his life. Perhaps

he was attracted to her in the light of the heroic dramas he was fond of - he had written a youthful novel, *Clisson et Eugénie*, whose hero died in battle rather than lose his wife's love - and perhaps also he wanted an older woman near him who could substitute in some way for his mother. He was clearly aware that 'Madame Mère' would not be best pleased to be supplanted, for when he and Josephine were married at a civil ceremony in Paris on 9 March 1796 neither she nor any others of the family was present, for they had not been told. Looking back, he himself said:

> My character made me naturally timid in (women's) company. Mme de Beauharnais was the first one who gave me any degree of confidence... One day when I was sitting next to her at table, she began to pay me all manner of compliments on my military qualities. Her praise intoxicated me. From that moment I confined my conversation to her and never left her side.

One way or another, they seem to have been well enough suited for the decade of marriage ahead; and anyway it was to be a decade in which Napoleon Bonaparte's preoccupations were with other matters than domesticity.

Two days after the marriage he left her for the first of many times - to take up his new post as Commander-in-Chief of the French Army of Italy.

Dynamic Leader

1796 – 1797

FRANCE WAS BANKRUPT, or virtually so. The Directory, needing to justify itself and divert the unhappy people's minds from dangerous notions of replacing it by some other form of dictatorship, wanted a glorious result to boast about. It also wanted plunder and means of keeping a substantial army in being without having to pay for it. The solution, propounded by Napoleon and certain other young officers thirsting for some fighting, was to sweep through Northern Italy and on into Austria, to gain a frontier on the Rhine, replenishing the national coffers in the process.

Pausing only to call on his mother and break the news of his marriage, which, as he had expected, was not at all well received, he arrived at his headquarters at the end of March 1796. Mutual disenchantment prevailed. His three divisional commanders were all considerably his senior in years and service, and were not pleased to greet him. He found the army in appalling shape, unpaid, poorly disciplined, its numbers much reduced by sickness and mutiny, and with more camp followers than soldiers occupying a line stretching almost from Nice to Genoa, about one hundred miles.

The soldiers themselves welcomed him, recognising a dynamic leader who might actually lead them somewhere. He proceeded to do this with an energy and efficiency which quickly won his officers over to him. Inside a fortnight he was driving inland from the coast, dividing and scattering the Austrian and Piedmontese forces facing him and notching up his first major victory in the battle of Montenotte on 12 April. Thousands were killed, and the French soldiers were able to make up from the dead their deficiencies in boots, clothing, weapons and supplies. What France could not afford to give them, victory under Napoleon had, leaving them eager for more. He did not disappoint them. There followed almost a battle a day - 13 April, Millesimo, 14 and 15, the first and second battles of Dego, 16-17, Ceva, 21st, Mondovi - and the French had broken through to the plains and were heading for Turin. It was the end of Piedmont: its King asked for peace, the Armistice of Cherasco was signed on 28 April, and looting and pillaging went into full swing, with wagon trains of booty heading back to France. Napoleon addressed his elated men:

> Soldiers! In fifteen days you have won six victories, taken twenty-one colours, fifty-five guns, several fortresses, and conquered the richest regions of Piedmont; you have taken 15,000 prisoners and killed or wounded more than 10,000 men.

He had done all that the Directory required of him, and more. Masterpieces of art - Leonardos, Michelangelos, Raphaels and Titians - as well as tons of other treasures of the Church and nobility and vast amounts of money poured back to Paris as the Army of Italy, now reinforced by the Army of the Alps, pressed on towards Milan. His men were by now of a mood to do anything for him. When Austrian guns and the muskets of three infantry battalions opposed the crossing of the 170-yard-long bridge over the River Adda at Lodi, mowing down more than three hundred Frenchmen, the grenadiers, led by Generals Massena and Berthier, still fought their way across. Milan fell within the week, and savage reprisals were exacted. The bridge at Lodi became a symbol of French heroism, indelibly associated with Napoleon's name, and put paid to the Directory's intention to divide command of the army between him and another general. 'Immortal glory to the conqueror of Lodi!' came the hasty response to his threat that he would resign rather than give up supreme command.

Despite the heady victories and rich plunder, so rapid an advance caused an over-extended line of communication for the relatively small army, whose handling of the populace had left few sympathisers in its wake. Proclamations about the brotherly treatment to be expected by those who behaved themselves were made mockery of by executions, hostage-taking, property-burning and rapine. Like many another conquering régime, the Directory had not the imagination to cultivate good relations with local political and social dissidents and enlist their aid in keeping the peace in the army's rear. Poor people as well as rich had been robbed and violated, while general outrage had been fermented by the desecration of churches and those neutral states which had been trespassed over in the advance. Guerrilla attacks grew to worrying proportions. Napoleon, who had nearly been trapped by a surprise incursion by Austrian cavalry into a village where he was dining, decided to provide himself with a personal bodyguard. It was a large one, comprising a squadron of cavalry and two battalions of grenadiers, in due course to become the famed and loyal Imperial Guard.

The ill-defended rear also offered a tempting opportunity to the Austrians to mount an encircling counter-attack. It came in July, in four columns totalling 47,000 men under 72-year-old Count Würmser. It had considerable success, causing even Bonaparte almost to panic, but he turned the tables on his aged adversary at Castiglione and drove him off with heavy losses.

Further counter-attacks by the superior Austrian army followed in the next weeks. The French army was more than ever depleted by sickness and casualties, and lacked all kinds of supplies. It nearly lost its commander-in-chief on 15 November when, during the battle of Arcola, he sought to rally his harassed men in yet another bridge crossing under withering fire. He leaped off his horse, seized a standard, and charged on to the bridge, shouting to them to follow. His alarmed aide-de-camp, Colonel Muron, pushed in front of him to shield him from the fire and received a fatal bullet which would otherwise have hit Napoleon. Tragedy gave way to near-comedy when another officer seized his general's coat-tails and tried to drag him back out of danger; Napoleon slipped and fell into the river mud. For all that, the resultant victory was another major one, costly in lives on both sides, but enhancing the enemy's respect for Napoleon as a fearless, quick-thinking commander, and restoring his self-esteem which always suffered when he was forced into defence or inactivity.

He began 1797 by winning another major battle at Rivoli (14 January) and took Mantua at last on 2 February. The way into Austria itself was now open to him. The Austrian army and his own lack of supplies might have stopped him, but his adversaries played into his hands by asking too quickly for an armistice. Napoleon promptly accepted and launched into peace negotiations without awaiting the Directory's instructions. The terms he granted were generous to Austria, which was already having second thoughts and might have decided to fight on, so the Treaty and Peace of Campo Formio were signed on 17 October 1797. From winning battles, Napoleon Bonaparte had gone on, through sheer skill, enterprise and personal example, to win a campaign. Still nearly three years short of thirty, '*le petit caporal*', as he was known to his ordinary soldiers, who liked to identify popular officers with their humbler ranks, had made of himself the hero figure which his bruised, confused nation so desperately needed.

Brilliantly successful in one campaign, he was less so in another. He had been obliged to leave Josephine two days after their marriage, and she was never wholly out of his mind, though he was very much out of hers. She had gained the security she wanted through marriage, but her inexperienced, gauche, though ardent bridegroom can hardly have provided much rapture. She, a natural Parisienne, was content to be in Paris, enjoying herself. She was interested in neither politics nor battles; she had seen quite enough danger and violence in the Revolution.

The long passionate letters Napoleon found time to write to her - one every day - evoked little response from her. When she answered them, which was not often, she made vague excuses for not going out to join him, as he repeatedly begged her to do. She feared war; she was not well; she might even be pregnant. This last item cheered Napoleon up greatly, but it was not true. In Paris she was dancing and dining, buying dresses and hats and running up bills.

Frustrated and disappointed, Napoleon began to suspect her constancy. He wrote bitterly:

> It seems to me you have chosen, and know where you can find my replacement. I wish you happiness, if unfaithfulness can bring it about - I say unfaithfulness, not perfidy. You have never loved me.

It was the kind of thing lovers say in the hope of hurting the beloved, not because they believe it. Unfortunately he had hit on the truth. Josephine had very quickly consoled herself for his absence with a handsome, dashing young cavalry officer, Louis Hippolyte Charles. When she finally came out to Italy in July 1796 she brought him with her.

Napoleon had set himself up in style at the castle of Montebello, near Milan, and here, while he was away fighting, she carried on the sort of life she had been leading in Paris, with Charles at her side. Gossip spread, which came to the ears of Napoleon. But he was happy, now that he had Josephine near him at last, happier, as it turned out, than he would ever be again, so he chose to ignore the rumours and put Josephine's unwise conduct down to her natural frivolity. Charles was tactfully dispatched back to Paris. But Josephine wrote to him with a warmth that was not to be found in her letters to her husband, and Napoleon was soon to write to Joseph, 'I have a great private sorrow; the veil has at last fallen from my eyes.'

The glorious victories of the past eighteen months had gained territory and treasure for France, but they had failed to win for the Directory the popularity which would enable it to go on controlling unchallenged the way of life of the French people. Eight years had passed since the Revolution, and it had become gradually obvious to ordinary men and women that they were no better off under five hard-faced Directors than they had been under one vacillating but well-meaning King. As with all dictatorships, it was only all right for those at the top. Wistful talk of 'the good old days' was increasingly heard and the Press becoming more daringly critical of the way things were going. To Napoleon Bonaparte, it sounded ominously like the voice of the despised mob again; and he knew how to deal with mobs.

This time there was no need of mayhem in the Paris streets. On his advice, and with the on-the-spot assistance of his 'proud brigand', the uncouth but valiant General Augereau, the *coup d'état* of 18 Fructidor An. V (4 September 1797) wiped out the forces of opposition at one stroke. Pending elections were cancelled, hostile newspapers were closed down, outspoken politicians were arrested and many of them banished to the colonies, and 15,000 armed soldiers under the man who had commanded the abortive invasion of Ireland the year before, General Hoche, stood by just in case. France was under martial rule.

Neatly timed to raise Parisian spirits, the Conquering Hero came home, to present the peace treaty to the Directory with his own hand. He was cheered, fêted, banqueted, and elected to the *Institut de France*, an honour he especially prized. There was another honour for him: on 16 October he was appointed to the command of the army to fight England.

Hero of Egypt

1797 – 1800

NAPOLEON'S NEW COMMAND was the most important his country had to offer. With Austria at least temporarily out ot the war, Italy and the Netherlands overcome, and Spain a relatively minor worry, Britain was the chief enemy. She was France's rival as the world's most prosperous trading nation and colonial power, an historic adversary and a monarchy that had given shelter to large numbers of French royalist *émigrés* from The Terror - and her prosperous, fertile land lay temptingly within sight of the French coast, little more than twenty miles distant.

The two countries had been at war since 1 February 1793, when Britain had become involved through her treaty with invaded Holland. Her army was small and weak, but the Royal Navy was the most powerful in the world, even though the area of its responsibility as protector of merchant shipping and far-flung possessions was very widespread. The French navy was large, too, but its efficiency and discipline were much eroded by unworkable efforts by the Revolutionary bureaucrats to impose equality among the sailors. The British tars, even though bad conditions caused them to mutiny briefly at Spithead and the Nore in 1797, remained dedicated to their ships, their country and their King.

While the Royal Naval blockade held France to near-famine conditions, the Directory desperately needed to strike some prestigious blow, and in

February 1797 made a reckless, unsuccessful attempt at a backdoor invasion at points on Britain's west coast. Frustrating as it was to a commander of Napoleon's mettle to know that he had only to get a firm footing on English soil to be certain of overwhelming her largely part-time army, he had to admit that the narrow strip of Channel presented an insurmountable obstacle.

> We cannot gain naval supremacy for some years to come. To invade England without that supremacy would be to embark on the most hazardous and difficult task ever attempted... If, in view of the state of our navy, it is impossible to act promptly, we can only abandon the expedition... As an alternative, we could undertake an eastern expedition in order to threaten England's trade with the Indies.

There was another option - to make peace. Britain herself had offered that, on quite reasonable terms, but Barras's hardline majority in the Directory refused. They wanted more than the return of a few captured colonies and England's recognition of France's new frontiers: they wanted Britain herself, and Napoleon thought he knew how that could be achieved.

Gibraltar was Britain's only naval base of consequence left in the Mediterranean, severely limiting the fleet's flexibility of movement and sources of supply. An 'eastern expedition', by which Napoleon meant an invasion of Egypt followed by an overland campaign on to India herself, would not only immediately replenish France's treasury still further and gain her priceless resources for the future, but would tie up the bulk of the Royal Navy on Mediterranean patrol. That in turn would leave England exposed to invasion, or force her to accept peace on France's terms.

It was not a new idea, but it seemed the best one available, and Napoleon was the type of person needing always to be getting on with things and trying something new. On 12 April 1798 he was appointed C-in-C Army of the Orient. Millions of francs were made available to enable an armada of warships and transports to leave Toulon and other ports next month, carrying an army of some 30,000 and all its equipment and supplies.

Napoleon sailed in the flagship *L'Orient*. Luck favoured him again. The assemblage of a fleet of more than 300 ships was no secret from London, but its destination was uncertain. A squadron commanded by Rear-Admiral Sir Horatio Nelson was dispatched from Gibraltar to investigate. A day or two sooner, and the sight of British sails approaching Toulon would have justified the misgivings of the French Admiral Brueys that the expedition was bound to be found by the Royal Navy and wiped out, and he would have refused to sail; but a gale dismasted Nelson's flagship, *Vanguard*, and the two fleets never saw one another. It was to take Nelson nearly three months' searching the Mediterranean for the elusive French.

There were several more near-misses before the French landed on Egyptian soil on 1 July. Alexandria was quickly taken and the usual ultimatum issued by Napoleon, offering the Egyptian people brotherhood or the sword. He lost no time in starting his advance up the Nile towards Cairo: a first glance had shown the dismayed French soldiery how little this hot and barren-looking land was likely to offer them in the way of loot or comfort. At least the fighting proved easier than in Europe, despite the ferocious aspect of the mounted Mamelukes. Modern artillery and firearms were too much for medievally-equipped horsemen and peasant infantry. The battle of the Pyramids (21 July) cost Napoleon only 300 casualties against some 5,000 Egyptians killed or wounded, and Cairo was in French hands.

Elation was soon turned to dismay. Nelson had found the French warships at last, anchored in what Admiral Brueys believed to be an impregnable position in Aboukir Bay at the mouth of the Nile. The British ships took advantage of penetrable gaps behind and between the French and destroyed almost all of them, Brueys perishing when *L'Orient* was blown to smithereens. It was more than a great Royal Naval victory: it meant that, deprived of naval support, Napoleon's Army of the Orient was marooned in Egypt, its supplies cut off. This served as the cue for renewal of hostilities against France by the European nations, joined this time by Russia and Turkey. It was as if with the cat, in the person of Napoleon Bonaparte, bottled up in the Middle East, the mice could come out and play.

The Egyptians under French occupation proved no more friendly than had the Italians, and the cut-off army's morale in an uncomfortable land sank. An uprising in Cairo was bloodily suppressed, but there was likelihood of further internal troubles and of a major attack from Turkish forces in Palestine. Napoleon resorted to the old device of taking his soldiers' minds off their grumbles, in this case by invading Syria in early 1799.

It was no walkover. He had to spend nearly a fortnight besieging the fortress of El Arish, stubbornly held by Albanians. When they at length surrendered they were paroled, only to turn up again at Jaffa, which Napoleon's army took by storm on 7 March. This time, although the garrison gave themselves up as prisoners of war, they were marched out and shot, more than two thousand of them. It was Napoleon's most monstrous massacre, the news of it serving to discredit further the Directory in the eyes of decent French people, although Napoleon had acted as his own master. Once more he resorted to a recklessly flamboyant act which might have cost him his life, in order to hearten his men. Plague was claiming many lives daily; Napoleon strode into the plague hospital, declaring that only those frightened of the dread disease could catch it, and carried out a victim's corpse to prove his point. His conduct on returning there in retreat a few weeks later was less heroic. He wanted the remaining survivors poisoned, but his chief medical officer flatly refused.

The chief reason for the retreat by the sick and hungry Army of the Orient was its defeat at the old Crusader fortress of Acre, the Turkish infantry base. With inadequate artillery Napoleon pounded away at the massive walls for two months, culminating in a reckless assault on foot which was thrown back with huge casualties. There was nothing for it but to fall back to Egypt; but Napoleon's personal luck was still on hand. When the Turks launched their own attack on 25 July with 8,000 men landed from British ships at Aboukir the French cavalry, led by the dashing Joachim Murat, routed them.

It was a timely success for Napoleon. He made up his mind to take advantage of it to return secretly to France. He sailed in a frigate from Alexandria in August, accompanied by his five chief generals, and after another narrow escape from the Royal Navy landed in France on 9 October, in nice coincidence with the publication of the reports of the victory at Aboukir. Thus he came home a hero.

He was not so much a hero as a menace in the Directory's eyes, however. Revolutionary fervour in France had waned by now. People were sick of war, of death, of famine, and of the rule of the 'five monkeys', as they had come to term Barras and his colleagues. The situation was ripe for a takeover, and the return of a people's hero spelled danger. Using invented rumours of a Jacobin plot as their excuse, the Directory prepared to transfer the seat of government from Paris to St Cloud, and placed Napoleon in charge of the troops drafted in to put down any demonstrations. His brother Lucien, president of the lower of the two legislative chambers, the Council of Five Hundred, invited Napoleon to address them. Seeing their hostility to him, Napoleon lost his temper.

> What has become of our glorious France? What have you done to her? I gave you victories; I find defeats. I sent you riches from Italy; I find crippling debts and destitution. What has become of the thousands of Frenchmen who were my friends, who shared my glory? They are dead!

He was mobbed by furious deputies, calling him a traitor. His brother called out to Murat, and with drums beating a section of fiercely-moustached grenadiers entered, to throw out those deputies who had not already thought it prudent to leave by the windows. It marked the end of the Directory and of the French Revolution. That same evening a Consulate of Three was declared, one of whom was Napoleon. Now only two other men were between him and sole dictatorship of the nation, which, in effect, was already his. A plebiscite gave overwhelming approval, and on 19 February 1800 the First Consul established himself in the royal palace of the Tuileries, once the home of the Bourbon kings. He was thirty years old, and the most powerful individual in Europe.

Emperor

1800 – 1807

AT LA MALMAISON, near Versailles, the country home of the First Consul and the First Lady of the land, the beautiful gardens contained a Temple of Love. Life at Malmaison was private and pleasant, but the couple who shared it might well have been already separated. While Napoleon had been away in Egypt the bored Josephine had returned to her old frivolous ways. Hippolyte Charles had come back into her life; at Malmaison, conveniently distant from Paris, they had amused each other. When rumours reached Egypt, Napoleon began to contemplate divorce.

When he got back to Paris the rumours were confirmed, and he heard for the first time about the debts she had incurred. She had gone to meet him, but her coach missed the way, and when she arrived in Paris he locked himself into his apartments, refusing to see her. Only her night-long entreaties outside his door, and the pleas of her two children, finally persuaded him to let her in. They were reconciled, but Josephine had weakened her own standing. She realised as much and began to behave herself; Hippolyte Charles was heard of no more at Malmaison.

Napoleon was by no means home for good, though, and there was still a little fighting to be done before he could set aside the sword for the pen and demonstrate to his people that a single genius at their head was worth any number of consuls, and that instead of thinking in terms of periodic elections and plebiscites they might as well settle for him outright. Appointing himself commander of the Army of the Reserve, in May 1800 he led a Hannibal-like march across the Alps, by way of the St Bernard Pass, intending to crush the Austrian army by surprise attack from the rear.

It almost proved a disaster. Over-confidence led him to underestimate the strength of the opposition and he manoeuvred two divisions away from the main force, never anticipating its coming under Austrian attack. When it did, near Marengo on 14 June, he would not at first believe it to be more than a bluff, but soon found his army suffering heavy casualties, running short of ammunition and seeming on the point of breaking ranks. His luck this time was in the person of General Louis Charles Desaix, a recently released prisoner of the British, who heard the guns at Marengo and came galloping back with his detached division, in time to save the day and transform a near-rout into a costly but splendid victory for the First Consul. Conveniently for Napoleon, Desaix was killed in the fighting, leaving him free to appropriate all the credit for this most important victory, which led the way to Austria suing for peace.

Britain was left alone in the field once more, Russia having retired from the fray. There remained the Royal Navy, though, and the British Army was improving and growing. It had its first battle with the French Army at Alexandria on 21 March 1801, following an immaculate combined-operation invasion of Egypt, and won, going on to liberate that country. But the general fact remained: Britain ruled the waves and France the land mass of Europe. In such stalemate conditions the Treaty of Amiens was signed on 25 March 1802, and what passed for peace settled on both lands.

The French people were duly thankful, after their seemingly endless years of strife, deprivation and persecution. They had found a father-figure whom they could trust to defend them with his genius in battle and whose instinct for their needs and desires seemed to extend to all spheres. By coming to terms with the Pope he had restored them to the Catholic communion, and now he set about reforming their laws under the *Code Napoléon*, which survives as today's *Code Civil*. He revised the administration, the tax laws, the educational system, the currency, and generally cleared up the mess left by successive dictatorships of corrupt and unpopular men, much of whose time had been spent at loggerheads with one another. Little wonder that he was eagerly voted Consul for life.

One obvious way to get rid of a nuisance possessing a lifelong mandate is to kill him. Several plots were hatched against Napoleon by frustrated royalists, the failure or exposure of each serving to increase public sympathy for him and add to the pressure for him to create a dynasty. Napoleon was by no means averse to putting on a crown and setting about founding a ruling line. On 18 May 1804, by popular request, he let himself be proclaimed Emperor. 'I accept the title you have thought advantageous to the glory of the nation,' was his reply to the Senate's offer. The good of the country was one and the same thing as his own happiness, he added.

Other titles flew: Joseph and Louis became princes, Letizia Bonaparte was exalted to *'Altesse Imperiale, Madame, Mère de l'Empereur'*. The arrangements for the Coronation ceremony were an all-important preoccupation. To persuade the Pope to officiate, Napoleon went through a religious ceremony of marriage with Josephine. Her worries that she might be discarded for barrenness were allayed by a decree that Napoleon's successor need not be a child of his marriage, but could be an adopted son - even one born out of wedlock - or a male heir of either Joseph or Louis, though not Lucien, who in 1803 had married a businessman's widow against Napoleon's wishes and refused either to divorce her or to accept royal honours, preferring exile in Rome. An emblem was chosen for the Bonaparte dynasty to oust the fleur-de-lis of the Bourbons: it was, appropriately, a bee, the one that had been found in the tomb of Chilperic, Merovingian King of the Franks. The sword of Napoleon's hero, Charlemagne, was brought from Aix-la-Chapelle.

The Coronation took place on 2 December 1804 in the Cathedral of Notre Dame. Napoleon was a glittering figure almost pulled down by the weight of his robes of velvet, silk and lace, and the jewels encrusting them. On his head was a laurel-wreath. With his peculiar flair for symbolism and drama, at the climax of the ceremony, after the Pope's blessing, Napoleon seized the crown from him, raised it and placed it symbolically on his own head. He then crowned Josephine with the smaller crown of the Empress. It was his supreme moment of triumph.

He and Josephine were living in the Tuileries, with Malmaison their private residence. But it was no time for domesticity. On the Champ-de-Mars, where stood the *École Militaire* of his cadet days, Napoleon presented his army with new colours, each standard surmounted with an imperial golden eagle, modelled on the standards of the Roman legions. Among military exercises, the splendour of new uniforms and martial music, he commanded his men to swear that they would rally to the eagles whenever their Emperor called, defend them with their lives, sustain them with their courage.

That rallying-cry would not be long coming. The Peace of Amiens was already at an end by the time Napoleon assumed his crown. It had become obvious to Britain that he was using the truce to mass and train his armies. He was building new warships, while Britain had cut her naval expenditure. He had banned trade between Britain and France, and was continuing his territorial expansion in Europe by taking over Switzerland and more of Italy. On 17 May 1803 Britain declared that the war was on again.

Napoleon did not understand the British character. To him England was *une nation de boutiquiers*, fecklessly made up of layered classes and multitudinous opinions, without feeling for *la gloire*, and with ideas of liberty idiosyncratically differing from those of France. Nevertheless, victory over that obdurate people represented an inestimable prize, and he determined once more to invade, this time with a vastly greater armada. His 'Project of England' was to involve 150,000 soldiers, whom he began massing on the Channel coast, with Boulogne as their main camp. Hundreds of barges were assembled, and with the coming of 1805 his admirals were receiving orders that the widely scattered French Navy should unite against Nelson.

Nelson, who had spent a boring summer of 1804 with none of the sea-fights he had hoped for, and an even more boring winter in ignorance of the whereabouts of the French and Spanish fleets, was delighted on 19 January 1805 to be signalled by his look-out frigate that 'the enemy is at sea'. Napoleon's scheme to get control of the Straits of Dover was to summon twenty French ships from Brest, ten from Toulon, and five from Rochefort, and add to them Spain's fifteen serviceable ships. Avoiding action, they were to proceed to the French arsenal Martinique and demolish British possessions in the area, thus distracting the British fleet's attention to that part. Then they would combine to cross the Atlantic and appear suddenly in the English Channel, whose remaining defences would be easily dealt with, while troops were landed in Ireland and the main body of men deposited on the English coast. Fear of invasion, which had been nervously awaited for over a year, would lead to swift capitulation on the part of the English and the eagle standards would soon wave triumphantly over the fields of Kent.

It was not to work out like that. Nelson, in H.M.S. *Victory*, led the fleet of ships which had followed him fruitlessly during 1804 on a 4,000-mile chase after the French. His sailors were highly trained professionals, contrasted with the uncoordinated amateurs who manned the French ships. Admiral Villeneuve sadly reported his men's inexperience and unreadiness to face storms and combat. Napoleon accused him of cowardice, and Villeneuve sailed from Cadiz, where his ships had taken shelter. The British were waiting for them. The confrontation came on 21 October 1805 off Cape Trafalgar, where Nelson destroyed the Franco-Spanish fleet without the loss of a single ship, though at the cost of his own life.

It was the end of a landsman's fantasy, a restless

dreamer's refusal to face facts. 'I cannot be every-where,' Napoleon fumed, and turned back to the element where he was at home, the land, seizing Vienna and luring the Austro-Russian armies to attack him near Austerlitz on 2 December, the first anniversary of his Coronation. The terrain was of his choosing, and his opponents accorded so obligingly with his tactics that it was as though he had been directing both sides in a classic, though bloody, exercise. 'The Russians and Austrians are destroyed,' he wrote to Josephine, adding one of his few record-ed expressions of human compassion for the dead and wounded of his own or his enemies' armies.

The Third Coalition of the Allies was in ruins, and Britain stood virtually alone yet again, though no longer in danger of invasion. In October 1806 Napoleon beat the veteran Field Marshal Blücher at Jena, a heavy defeat for Prussia. Never mind Perfidious Albion: he could feel himself to be truly Master of Europe. Austria had ceded to him the mainland territories of Venice, and all her possess-ions in Germany. French troops swarmed over the Papal States and the Kingdom of the Two Sicilies, where Napoleon had created a Kingdom of Naples and in March 1806 set his brother Joseph over it as monarch. That January he had married Josephine's son Eugène Beauharnais to the Elector of Bavaria's daughter, created Louis King of Holland, and Jerome King of the new state of Westphalia, part of Germany. Jerome's rash love-match with the beau-tiful Miss Betsy Patterson of Baltimore was swiftly annulled by his brother, infuriated that Jerome should presume to ally himself with a commoner and an American, however rich and lovely. Napo-leon found a more suitable wife for him, Princess Catherine of Würtemberg.

Louis was already married (suitably, in Napo-leon's eyes) to Hortense Beauharnais, Josephine's daughter. The marriage was a disaster, but Napo-leon, who had always had an undeservedly high opinion of Louis, wished to adopt the first child, Louis Napoleon, and make him his heir. Joseph had two daughters but no sons; Jerome, as yet, no children by his second wife. Male heirs were scarce for founding a dynasty.

In December 1806 an important thing happened: Napoleon's mistress Éleanore Denuelle Revel, who was employed in the household of the Princess Caroline Murat, Napoleon's sister, gave birth to a son. It was not her husband's, but Napoleon's. At last he knew that Josephine's infertility was not his fault. He was still writing to her, 'There is only one woman for me... the nights are long here, alone...'; but the birth of Charles Léon turned his attention to other possibilities.

Less than a month later he met and instantly fell in love with the Countess Marie Walewska. He was adding Poland to his conquests at the time, and when he made his entry into Warsaw on New Year's Day 1807 the beautiful, graceful Marie came to welcome him and made more of an impression than she had intended. He wooed her hotly, in vain at first. Only when persuaded by her husband and other nobles that her surrender would be to Poland's advantage did she capitulate, and became genuinely fond of Napoleon, becoming known as 'the Emperor's Polish Wife'. She bore him an illegitimate son, Alexandre Florian Joseph, in 1810, with unhappy consequences for the Emperor's French Wife, Josephine.

The Dynast

1807 – 1811

A CARTOON OF 1807 depicts Napoleon straddling a globe. All Europe is beneath him, but just beyond his reach lies a little territory labelled 'Old England', from which a diminutive John Bull is hacking at the Emperor's left foot with a tiny sabre.

He had tried and tried to overcome Great Britain, but was still no closer to succeeding. For all her smallness, she was the paymaster of the nations, the most influential colonial and trading power, and her navy reigned supreme. As he had long ago recognised, Napoleon had to destroy that naval might; and events in 1807 seemed to offer him the means of doing it.

He had scored a series of major victories over the armies of Prussia and Russia, causing both to seek peace. Napoleon saddled Prussia with harsh terms, including the closure of her ports to British trade. He was less harsh with Russia, but met the Tsar Alexander I in a spirit of friendship on an elaborately appointed barge on the Niemen River at Tilsit on 25 June 1807, noting with satisfaction the Tsar's opening words: 'I hate the English as much as you do. I am ready to help you against them in any way.' Napoleon was moved to respond, 'Friendship between France and Russia has been my most cherished dream.' During their fortnight of talks they cemented their understanding into a treaty of alliance, one of whose provisions was that Russian ports, too, would no longer admit British merchant shipping.

Napoleon saw the way to success against his most persistent enemy. If he could deprive Britain of enough of her overseas trade, and at the same time use the might of the new alliance to force weaker countries to hand over warships, Britain would be bankrupted and the Royal Navy overwhelmed by sheer numbers. It was agreed between the two Emperors that Russia should deal with Sweden, and France with Denmark and Portugal.

It was a perfect plan, except that it did not work. Somehow, word of it leaked, and for once the British Government acted decisively and fast. British ships and troops were sent to Copenhagen, and when the Danes refused to surrender their fleet their capital was bombarded and their ships were sailed away to England or burnt where they lay. Sweden took the hint and refused to part with her fleet to Russia, while Portugal hesistated long enough for a British squadron to take up station at the mouth of the River Tagus, sealing off the exit for nine Russian men-o'-war which had sailed in to shelter from storms and were not particularly anxious to leave. Napoleon's plan to outnumber the Royal Navy had failed.

He invaded Denmark and Portugal, however, and so was able to close off many ports, including those from which Britain received her all-important supplies of shipbuilding timber. Otherwise, the well developed smuggling system between Britain and Europe stayed open for business as usual, and trade suffered little. And then, having failed in one of his brightest schemes, Napoleon made one of his biggest mistakes: he decided to occupy Spain.

It was a reckless, ill-considered move by an impatient man who believed that he had only to set a thing into motion and it would somehow be achieved. In effect, he tied up a third of a million men of the *Grande Armée* in the enterprise and many of the warships he needed so badly. He misjudged the strength of Spanish patriotism and their resentment of plundering interlopers who showed consideration neither for their persons and possessions, nor for their venerated religious houses, with their

holy treasures. When a riot by protestors in
Madrid in May 1808 was turned into a massacre by
the French commander, Murat, equally bloody
massacres erupted throughout Spain, with the
French as their victims. Murat, who was Napoleon's
brother-in-law, was soon afterwards stricken with
ill-health. Napoleon ordered his brother Joseph to
hand over the Kingship of Naples to Murat and
take over the Spanish Throne. (The reluctant
Joseph lasted only three weeks in Madrid before
quitting its dangers for the relative safety of Vitoria,
the headquarters of the *Armée de l'Espagne*.) But
the situation of the French army in Spain was serious everywhere: recognising at last that this conquest was to be no walkover, Napoleon decided
that he had better take charge himself.

> I take my leave in a few days to place myself at the
> head of my army, and, with God's help, I shall
> crown the King of Spain in Madrid and place my
> eagles on the ramparts of Lisbon... It is the
> special blessing of Providence, which has always
> watched over our armies, to have blinded the
> English into leaving the protection of the sea and
> at last exposing their troops on the land.

After years of war and tardy development of an
efficient army, trained to the highest standard of
musketry by Sir John Moore at Shorncliffe Camp
on the Kentish coast, Britain had seen and seized
the opportunity to commence land operations
against France by coming to the aid of an old ally,
Portugal. Sir John Moore's expeditionary force
was small, and over-reached itself in trying to link
up with Spanish troops in Spain itself and drive the
French out. It was the one to be driven out early in
1809, with heavy losses, Moore among them; but it
had been initiated in battle, and had learned many
lessons to add to his training, and Napoleon fatally
under-estimated its resilience when he returned to
France within a matter of weeks, asserting that
there would be no more trouble over Spain.

Returned to Paris, he set about another attack on
Austria, where a new spirit of insurrection had

arisen. A partly-conscripted army, of poor quality, the Army of the Rhine, was sent to war against the much more professional Austrian army. On 9 April the Austrian forces, under Archduke Charles, invaded France's ally Bavaria. In the struggle that ensued Napoleon's troops threw them back, and marched towards Vienna; but Archduke Charles was waiting, and on 21 May his 100,000 Austrians drove the French out of Aspern and Essling, forcing Napoleon to withdraw. He had suffered a downright, unquestionable defeat, losing over 20,000 men and Marshal Lannes, an old comrade-in-arms.

On 5 and 6 July he had his full revenge at the Battle of Wagram, at the cost of shattering his army's nerve and losing 23,000 men killed and wounded, 7,000 missing. On 12 July an armistice was signed, on 14 October the Franco-Austrian war was ended by the Treaty of Schönbrunn.

Napoleon by this time, entering his forties, had changed into a man unrecognisable from the earlier portraits of him as a lanky, hollow-cheeked scarecrow, the image beloved of English caricaturists. From his middle thirties he had been getting rapidly plumper, round-faced and square-jawed, his hair very dark and short, the eyes duller, almost sleepy, the body stout on puny legs. It was not an attractive transformation. He himself said that it was due to 'campaigning, agitating and movement', and the frequent hot baths to which he was addicted cannot have slimmed him at all. He was not given to over-eating, or indeed at all interested in food, which he was in the habit of bolting so rapidly that nobody at the table could keep up with him. Wine also failed to interest him, and it has been suggested by medical men that he may have had some form of pituitary malfunction.

He was conscious of the passage of time, increasingly aware of the importance of founding a dynasty. It seemed unlikely to be provided by his unsatisfactory brothers, therefore he himself must get an heir. Josephine had despaired of giving him one. In 1809 she was forty-six, all medical remedies having failed to make her fertile. She knew of Éleanore

Revel's son, and of Marie Walewska's pregnancy, and she also knew that as far back as 1807 her husband had begun to draw up lists of eligible princesses who might provide him with 'a womb', as he realistically put it. Alarmed, she had written to her children for advice, to be told by her son Eugène:

> He must treat you well, give you an adequate settlement and let you live in Italy with your children. The Emperor will then be able to make the marriage which his policy and his happiness demand... If the Emperor wishes to have children who are truly his, there is no other way.

So prepared, it cannot have come altogether as a shock to her when on 30 November 1809 Napoleon broke the news of his intention to divorce her. He did it in the traditional manner, over the dinner-table. He laid out his reasons logically: the welfare of the State and the future of the Empire depended on his marriage to someone fertile. He assured her that he loved her and that she had been a good wife to him, which was true - her grace and charm had helped to make up for his lack of them, her sophistication for his sense of social inferiority. He was generous enough to say that he loved her still, and this was no doubt true. Their years of marriage had bound them in a relationship of mutual affection and loyalty; but it was not enough, with such great things at stake.

Josephine did not take the news meekly. She wept and protested, she appealed to his feelings for her as a husband, to the memory of their years together, knowing all the time that her pleas were useless, and soon she would be alone, deserted, no longer an Empress. Storms of emotion at last dissolved in tears and collapse. Instead of taking her in his arms, Napoleon called the prefect of the Tuileries and ordered that she be carried downstairs to her own rooms. On 15 December the ceremony of divorce took place in the Tuileries. Tearfully holding Josephine's hand, Napoleon read out the Imperial declaration of divorce, a decree of State signed by them both. Then he withdrew to his own apartments, in perfectly genuine distress.

Josephine had nothing to complain of in the settlements he made for her. She had two million francs a year, a Paris home in the Elysée Palace, the country home at Malmaison, and a hunting-box at Navarre. Her favourite home was Malmaison, a house of great charm in spite of its name, set in beautiful gardens. Gardening was Josephine's passion: the Malmaison rose is for ever associated with her name. On the estate of 300 acres there were not only gardens, but farms and an extraordinary menagerie of animals and birds including parakeets, chamois, kangaroos, an ostrich, a seal, and other exotic creatures besides the more usual domestic animals and dogs. In all probability she was contented enough. Napoleon never broke his ties with her, insisted that she maintain Imperial state, and kept her in touch with important people. When she died in 1814, possibly of diphtheria, she was genuinely mourned, for she had been genuinely liked.

In Napoleon's urgent search for a second bride he had cast hopeful glances towards two sisters of the Tsar, but received only polite excuses, which did nothing to further Franco-Russian relations. He then settled for the Archduchess Marie Louise, eldest daughter of the Emperor of Austria, his recent bitter enemy. Such a union would unite Austria and France, and Marie Louise seemed a hopeful candidate for Imperial motherhood. She was eighteen, a large pink-and-white blonde, whose mother, grandmother and great-grandmother had all been extremely fertile. She had led a very sheltered life in the prim atmosphere of the Austrian Court, her favourite companions pet ducks (females only), her main hobby eating cream-cakes, and she had no intellectual pretensions. Napoleon approved of submissive women, and was excited at the thought of marrying such a young one. He did his best to smarten himself up for her, even learning the new fashionable waltz. He was immensely proud, too, that his bride belonged to one of the grandest royal families of Europe.

After the wedding on 1 April 1810 he watched her

like a hawk, mindful of Josephine's infidelities in the early years of his first marriage, but Marie Louise was not at that time interested in men. He also treated her with respect and consideration, just a little overawed by her royal status, contrasted with his own. She remarked in a letter to Metternich, the Austrian Chancellor, not long after the marriage, that she was not afraid of her husband, but was beginning to think he was afraid of her.

The main object of the match was soon achieved. On 20 March 1811, nine months after the marriage, Marie Louise produced a son, Napoleon-François-Joseph-Charles. The heir was in the cradle, the guns of Paris fired salutes; the omens seemed propitious. The baby was immediately given the title of King of Rome. Napoleon was thrilled and delighted at the fulfilment of his hopes, and adored his little son. A sketch made when the child was about two shows him lying asleep on a couch, his head on his father's knee, in an attitude of utter trust; he was always to remember Napoleon with fondness and loyalty. The little King of Rome was a fair, pretty child, very like his mother, with a bright mind, and no sign so far of the tragic future which lay in wait for him.

Russian Roulette

1812 – 1814

IN INVADING SPAIN, Napoleon had made the cardinal mistake of underestimating his opponents' courage and the hostility of the occupied populace. He made the same mistake when he came to turn on Russia; only this time there were more disastrous consequences, for it was only one of many major miscalculations.

In spite of their pronouncements of friendship and mutual loyalty and aid made at Tilsit in 1807, renewed and expanded in a further meeting at Erfurt the following year, he and the Tsar were not close allies. Tsar Alexander, a suspicious, unstable man, recognised his supposed partner as someone not to be trusted, subject to sudden whims and capable of anything that would serve his own ends. Napoleon regarded himself as the commanding figure in the partnership, and the Tsar of all the Russias naturally resented it.

When Napoleon was drawing up his list of replacements for Josephine, he had put at the top of it the name of the Tsar's young sister Anna. Her brother's approval was not forthcoming, and Anna married the Duke of the German state of Oldenburg, which Napoleon proceeded to seize in 1811. Having meanwhile married Marie Louise, princess of Austria, that very country which he and the Tsar had pledged to fight against together, Napoleon doubly displeased his Russian friend and gave proof that he was not to be trusted.

Napoleon's insistence on a ban on trade with Britain remained another sore point with Russia, whose own commerce suffered severely from it. There were old ties between Britain and Russia - the Russian navy was largely modelled on the Royal Navy and trained by its officers - and before long the trading links were resumed, to Napoleon's fury. These and other specific grievances, along with the mutual mistrust and Napoleon's overbearing attitude towards his ally, fermented in his endlessly scheming mind and produced an intoxicating notion: he would teach Russia a lesson by the means he knew best.

His genius lay, after all, in his ability to command in the field. His broader machinations were less successful, due to his inability to foresee consequences and his anxiety to get moving on each new enterprise. In spite of certain physical afflictions which made horse-riding painful to him, he was keen to get back into the saddle and direct new victories; and, as he saw it, one or two good trouncings would quickly have the Tsar bending the knee to him.

He gave his usual impatient orders for a huge army to be assembled. Half a million men were to make up the *Grande Armée*, with more than a thousand artillery pieces, tens of thousands of horses and oxen, and immense quantities of supplies and wagons. He did not expect to have to penetrate very far into Russia before forcing a surrender, but he correctly guessed that there would be little food for his men or forage for his beasts to be picked up on the way, so several weeks' supplies must be taken. As it turned out, these proved severely inadequate. The army, made up of many nationalities, and its huge attendance of women and other camp followers, was hungry before it even marched into Russia, while there were already more sick than the scant and poorly organised medical facilities could cope with.

The responsibility was Napoleon's. He could not adequately delegate authority to others. He had to plan and oversee everything himself, from strategy and tactics to logistics and the commissariat.

This time the task was simply too great for him. The *Grande Armée* which marched against Russia in 1812 constituted the biggest military undertaking in history so far; and the supreme egotist who had called it into being, and prepared it, and launched it towards its doom was by now, although he would have been the last to see or concede it, starting to lose his touch and his luck.

His greatest asset remained a moral one - the loyalty of his men. Even the foreigners who marched under his command were confident that anything he undertook must turn out a success, while his French troops, especially the leathery old veterans of his diverse campaigning, simply loved him. Though they had seen hundreds of thousands of their comrades killed and maimed to further his ambition - he enjoyed taking a stroll among the carnage after a battle - they were willing to go on laying their own lives on the line for him. Not only willing, but eager: he possessed that rare mesmeric appeal which drives fighting men to feats beyond their physical and psychological endurance, to the consternation of their opponents who wonder what else they must do to stop them.

The advance was a shambles, though; a chaos of marching feet, plodding hooves, grinding wheels, in foul weather and with rations short from the start. It was slow-moving, grossly unwieldy, over the dreadful roads of Poland. The Niemen river was crossed on 24 June and they lumbered on to Russian earth, to find it 'scorched' by the fleeing inhabitants to deny them shelter and any hope of supplies. Instead of massing to oppose them, the Russian army kept withdrawing, letting them advance further and further into their inhospitable territory. This was not some masterly plan, however; it was due to irresolution amongst the Russian higher command and chaotic differences of opinion. Ironically, though, the very lack of a pitched battle was achieving as much as the Russians might have hoped for had they offered one. The *Grande Armée* left a thick trail of dead men, women and horses and abandoned equipment in its wake. It spent nearly three months straggling forward into Russia, exhausting itself as it went and losing half its numbers through sickness, starvation and exposure, and from increasing attacks by partisan guerrillas, before the Russians at last stood up and fought it at the village of Borodino, on the Kaluga river, about 70 miles from Moscow itself.

It was a bloody slogging match between two exhausted armies of roughly equal strength, equally badly directed. Napoleon was unwell and sullenly uncommunicative; two of the Russian generals were not even on speaking terms. By the time neither side had any strength left to go on fighting, and the Russians withdrew, some 80,000 men in all had fallen. The token victory for Napoleon enabled him to ride into Moscow a week later, on 13 September. 'Peace lies in Moscow. When the grand Russian nobles see us masters of their capital they will think twice before continuing the war,' he had declared. In fact, the Russians had every intention of continuing, and the city he occupied was an empty one, deserted and half-stripped . He had no sooner established himself in the Kremlin than fires broke out in several other parts, burning down three-quarters of the city.

It was hint enough that there was to be no surrender. The French army was far from its homeland, with nothing behind it but empty wilderness and nothing to go on for; and it was October, with the bitter Russian winter coming. The retreat from Moscow was ordered. By 4 November the snow was falling.

The withdrawal was a pathetic tragedy. Starved and ragged, they froze where they lay down or fell. Napoleon, with his blind confidence, had not thought to establish a chain of supply depots on which they might fall back. And all along the way they struggled they were pursued by the Cossacks, raided and attacked. The Russians strove to trap the entire army, and almost succeeded. The bridge across the River Beresina, forming the border between Russia and Poland, was destroyed, but by mid-November the river should have been frozen solid anyway. Instead, a sudden thaw had melted the ice, leaving a rushing torrent. Incredible work

by the engineers under General Eblé, working up
to their waists in the icy water for hours at a time,
resulted in two bridges being built from the tim-
bers of nearby houses. Though these came under
Russian artillery fire, and one was twice destroyed,
some 25,000 men got across. They and a few thousand who struggled out of Russia by other routes
were all that remained of the *Grande Armée*.

Legend has it that the last Frenchman to leave
Russian soil was Marshal Michel Ney, commander
of the rearguard during the retreat's most crucial
phase. The principle that a sinking ship's captain
should be the last to leave her does not apply to
supreme commanders of armies in retreat. Napoleon reached safety, and, as when things had gone
wrong in Egypt, decided he had urgent business in
Paris. In fact, he had, for there had been an
attempted coup against his régime, led by a General Malet who had put word about that Napoleon
had died in Russia, thereby spreading alarm and
confusion. It was important for the Emperor to
show himself and reassert his authority, as he told
General Murat when handing over to him:

> I can only retain my grasp on Europe from the
> Tuileries. I must keep an eye on Austria and see
> that Prussia stays loyal. When they know I am
> back in Paris, leading the nation and at the head
> of the 200,000 men I shall raise, they will think
> twice before they go to war against me.

It was an echo of what he had said about invading
Russia, with similar tones of almost maniacal over-
confidence; yet it is a measure of the man, and of
his people's total faith in him, that, by the end of
April 1813, the new army had been raised. It was
by no means a Grand Army; a great part of it was
found through harsh conscription, with the age of
its soldiers becoming ever lower. It was also de-
ficient in cavalry, who took much longer to train
than infantry, and in horses to replace the thousands lost. But Napoleon could still win battles
against the Prussians, seizing their chance to get
rid of France from her territories. Lützen and

Bautzen were two heartening successes for him in May, forcing another armistice in June; and when that broke down in August he won a major battle at Dresden against a quarter of a million Austrians and Russians, losing only one man for every four opponents.

But all his old enemies were by now seeing him as a savage dog at bay. Coalitions were springing up right and left. In Europe, that of Austria, Prussia and Russia brought together so many fighting men that the battle of Leipzig, from 16-18 October, was dubbed the 'Battle of Nations', with more combatants than took part in any other single action of the entire Napoleonic Wars. It cost him 73,000 casualties and control of Germany. A setback of that magnitude was more than even his resilience could stand up to, especially since it threw him on to the defensive, which was not his style - and the territory he had to defend was France itself. From now on, the battles on the Continent of Europe would bear French names. They continued to be hard fought, though. Such notions as the more optimistic of the Allies had of racing to Paris within a week or two were thwarted by a series of dashing actions under Napoleon's own direction.

All this time, large numbers of French soldiers had remained tied up in the Spanish enterprise. Portugal had remained a stubborn stronghold of resistance, and a tactician worthy to match Napoleon himself, though with more patience, had emerged in Arthur Wellesley, Duke of Wellington, who was gradually building up a combined British-Portuguese-Spanish army, aided by organised guerrillas and with the advantage of a highly developed intelligence service. Following the losses suffered in Sir John Moore's campaign, strong reinforcements of cavalry and infantry had been shipped in from England, and with a winter of hardening and acclimatising behind them they moved on to the offensive early in 1813 with easy superiority of numbers and morale against the forces commanded by the reluctant King Joseph Bonaparte. A series of hard sieges and battles culminated in his defeat at Vitoria (21 June 1813) and the chase of the disorganised French across the

Pyrenees and into their home country.

Again, it proved no walkover to occupy France. Napoleon's loyal Marshal Soult, who had chased Moore's army out of Spain and for a time has aspired to the crown of Portugal, held up the invaders for almost a year. All the time, though, he was losing ground to the implacable Wellington, standing finally at Toulouse on 10 April 1814. Before Soult evacuated the town next evening some eight thousand men of both sides had been killed or wounded - needlessly, as it turned out, for on 6 April, unknown to the combatants in this theatre of war, Napoleon had abdicated.

Elba and Back

1814 – 1815

NAPOLEON ABDICATED ON Easter Monday, 11 April 1814. In his own hand he wrote down his renunciation, on his own behalf and that of his heirs, of all claims to the thrones of France and Italy. The Allies accepted, but on their own terms. Napoleon might still call himself Emperor, but he must live in exile on the island of Elba, off the west coast of Italy. Two million francs a year were to be shared between him and Marie Louise.

He refused the terms. Left alone with the document, he gave way to despair; at midnight on 12 April he attempted suicide by poison. One of his valets saw him take the draught and called his principal valet, Constant, who noticed on the floor the remains of a purse or sachet which Napoleon had carried ever since the Egyptian campaign - as a talisman, Constant had always thought, but evidently it had been a poison kept for just such a moment as this. Either he had miscalculated the dose, or the poison was ineffectual. By next morning he was better, ready to sign the agreement. A week later he left Fontainebleau for Elba. At Fontainebleau they still pluck tourists by the sleeve and point out the courtyard of the White Horse, where he said an emotional farewell to all that were left of his Imperial Guard. There was nobody else to bid him farewell. Marie Louise had fled with her small son to Rambouillet; he would never see either of them again. Josephine was at Malmaison, seriously ill, and was to die within a few weeks. Joseph and Jerome had fled to Switzerland, as had Louis; the others were variously scattered. Only Marie Walewska, ever faithful, had visited Napoleon at Fontainebleau, but he was too distrait to see her, and she quietly went away.

As he journeyed south to the coast with his entourage, in the first of fourteen carriages, the crowds at first cheered him, then, the further south he went, the cheers turned to boos and showers of stones. When he reached Avignon on 26 April he found the mood of the people ugly. Filth, as well as stones, was flung at his carriage, and he saw effigies of himself hanging from improvised gibbets. At a coaching inn a servant-girl, not recognising him or pretending not to, described to him with relish what the citizens of Avignon would do to the Emperor once they got their hands on him - it would be a lynching to remember. He who had never been a coward in war was shaken by civilian vindictiveness and the possibility of a humiliating death. He disguised himself as an Englishman, with the improbable name of Lord Berghersh, and later in the journey as an Austrian officer. At Le Luc his sister Pauline was waiting to see him, and managed to put him back in spirits. Then he travelled to the port of Fréjus, where the British frigate *Undaunted* was waiting. She arrived at Porto Ferrajo, Elba, on 4 May. Meanwhile, King Louis XVIII and his Court packed up their belongings at Hartwell House, near Aylesbury, Buckinghamshire, and thankfully ended five years' exile in England.

Life on Elba was pleasant enough. There was no guard over him, and apart from a British Commissioner he was virtual ruler of the island. But contentment and resignation were not in Napoleon's nature. His days were as full as he could make them - reviewing the Guard (he had been allowed to keep something like a thousand of the Old Guard, and his favourite horses), holding levées, and generally making the Governor wonder whether he ever sat down. He sported the new flag of Elba, designed by himself (a white ground, with three gold bees on red - B for Bonaparte). He inspected iron mines, in the hope of getting some income from them. He worked on the house he had been given, the Casa Mulini, making up for its inadequate furnishings by sending workmen to a villa owned by his sister Elisa, with orders to dismantle it and bring to his place anything worth having, including floor-boards and shutters. The rest of the furniture was provided from the costly belongings of his brother-in-law Prince Borghese, Pauline's husband, removed from a ship blown into Elba en route for Rome. Two guest suites were provided, one for Marie Louise, the other for their little son. But they remained empty. A woman and a child did arrive, and were mistaken for the ex-Empress and the ex-King of Rome, but they were Marie Walewska and her son. Pauline came to visit, and Madame Mère. Pauline enlivened the social life of Elba by getting Napoleon to play party games, and encouraging him to put live sardines into Bertrand's pockets.

All the time, throughout these mild amusements, Napoleon was thinking, planning. His mail was regularly searched by agents of the Allies, but he had his own methods of finding out what was going on; for instance, that Talleyrand, the head of France's provisional government, was trying to have him transferred to some less accessible island, and that the reinstated Bourbons were not popular in France. And now he made one of those massive, tragic miscalculations which had been his strategical weakness throughout his career. Feeling in Europe, and particularly France, had changed. Wars had gone on long enough; now the people wanted peace, not *la gloire*, constitutional rulers, not heroes. France was not ready for him to return, but return he must and would.

'France wants me back,' he told Elban authorities. 'The Bourbons have ruined my country.' Then he went to Mass with his mother and sister, arranged for the governing of Elba during his absence, gratefully accepted Pauline's gift of her diamonds, had the frigate *Inconstant* refitted and equipped for a three-month voyage, closed his accounts and drew up a military budget, collected together his Old Guard and other troops, and nonchalantly set sail, with seven ships, for France, reaching her shores on 1 March. It was his last throw of the dice.

It was true that the restored Bourbon monarchy was not popular. Louis XVIII, brother of the murdered King Louis XVI, was fifty-nine years old and so corpulent that he could not move without help. The rest of the family inspired no confidence either by their appearance or their manners. Parisians knew very little about them, and they had strong enemies; there had even been assassination plots. One of the most unpopular edicts the insensitive Louis had made up was the closure of inns and wineshops on Sundays. When he later returned to power he was no longer known as Louis le Desiré, but as Louis l'Inévitable. When the news of Napoleon's coming reached them the Bourbons shuffled out of Paris, rather than leaving with dramatic farewells.

Napoleon landed near Cannes on 1 March 1815. He had hardly set out from there for Paris when he became ill, and immediately had to abandon his horse and take to a carriage. The ailment was either the effects of an attack of cystitis, or pain from prolapsed haemorrhoids, both violently uncomfortable, the same trouble which had affected him at the Battle of Borodino. But in spite of not being able to undertake the classic triumphal march he had envisaged, he collected over fourteen thousand devoted adherents before he reached Paris. Many of those who had turned out to oppose him were won over by the old loyalties, and a last hope that he could prove to be the ruler they needed.

On 20 March he entered Paris, and was carried up the great staircase of the Tuileries on the shoulders of the crowd, smiling, his arms outstretched like someone sleepwalking or in a trance. At the Tuileries his stepdaughter Hortense was waiting. She and her ladies had spent the morning unpicking the Bourbon fleurs-de-lis which had been tacked over the Imperial bees on the carpets. The family, except for Louis, soon joined him. The 'Hundred Days' had begun.

He needed urgently to raise troops, but nine of his marshals refused to serve under him. He mustered conscripts of the class of 1815, untrained lads, and mobilised 230,000 of the National Guard to join his 25,000 veterans. Arms were scarce, like uniforms, and it was hard to get back the five thousand cavalry horses which had been hired out to farmers. There was widespread resentment of conscription, with uprisings here and there, and a general feeling of unease pervaded France as the shadow of new war crept up. He reigned alone, without his consort or his son, so that it was impossible to hold court, and he abandoned the Tuileries for the less formal Élysée. The news reached him that England had committed herself to spending five million pounds a year until he could be recaptured, and that Switzerland had closed her frontiers against France, Spain had declared war, and the British were sinking French shipping.

On 1 June was held the ceremony of the Champ de Mai, an occasion for the assembly of troops, the firing of guns, the display of eagle standards and state coaches. A large platform was built out from the *École Militaire*, and on this Napoleon, with his brothers Lucien, Jerome and Joseph, appeared dressed in full state costume. The crowds fell silent, staring at the costumes of white satin, ornamented with rosettes and diamonds, and purple cloaks trimmed with ermine. This unfortunate get-up, belonging to no known age or military style, was not helped by Napoleon's semi-audible speech, of which nobody seems to have heard much more than the words *'Empéreur, consul, soldat, je tiens tout du peuple.'* A few voices shouted *'Vive Marie Louise!'* to which there was really no answer.

On 7 June Napoleon attended the opening of the new French Parliament, looking ill and seeming unhappy with his declaration of himself as a constitutional monarch. On 11 June he dined with his family for the last time. Early next morning he left Paris to try to regain his lost empire.

The Hundred Days

1815

AFTER THE ABDICATION there had arisen the task of restoring equable order to the fragmented Europe lying scattered in the wake of a decade and a half of Napoleon Bonaparte. Nothing less than a summit conference of leading representatives of the principal powers involved could hope to achieve it, and this was duly convened to begin on 1 November 1814, named the Congress of Vienna, after that twice-captured crossroads of Europe at which it appropriately took place. It was a drawn-out occasion of celebratory social glitter, as well as earnest discussion and wrangling, and for all these reasons it was slow to reach its conclusions. It was still alternately debating and dancing when the news reached it of Napoleon's return. The horrified delegates packed up their papers and their dancing pumps, declaring him an outlaw, and their armies began re-mustering for war.

The latest, and last, of Napoleon's armies was called the Army of the North. One bold victory, Napoleon knew, would unite the French people behind him to fresh endeavours. The Duke of Wellington had gone back to London, to receive the tokens of his fame, while his forces had been to a large extent scattered, the British transferred to America to try to settle the tedious war which had been going on there since 1812, and the Spaniards repatriated as an undisciplined nuisance. The 'Iron Duke' was dispatched hastily back to the

Continent at the head of an Anglo-Dutch army which would link up with Blücher's Prussians, Wellington assuming overall command. Although numerically outnumbered, Napoleon had the advantage of experienced troops, compared with the heterogeneous and largely untried forces available to his two antagonists. If he could strike fast, he could hope to keep them apart and defeat them separately.

He tackled the Prussians first, on 15 June 1815, attacking their posts on the River Sambre and driving them back, intending to race to Brussels. Next day he attacked them with three divisions and the 'British' - there were only some 23,000 actual Britons among Wellington's 80,000 men - with two. He beat the Prussians at Ligny, but failed to follow up decisively. Brave old Blücher, who was 73 years old and had been about to retire from service when summoned back for this campaign, had been unhorsed and trampled on, but dosed himself liberally with his favourite gin and regrouped his men, determined to link up with Wellington, who was massing his army on high ground near the village of Waterloo. Napoleon, too, assembled his force on high ground less than a mile away. There, on the following morning, 18 June, he made the final mistake of his career.

His error was twofold: to assume that the Prussians he had left in defeat were out of the reckoning, and that Wellington's motley force was the proverbial sitting duck, certain to give way before a mass onslaught. In fact, Blücher was making all haste to come to the support of his ally and friend; it was a question only of whether Wellington could hold out meanwhile. He might not have managed, had Napoleon not been suffering a particularly excruciating attack of piles, which, together with weariness and general debility, dulled his mind. Instead of making his attack in several-pronged formation, he threw in his divisions in a frontal mass. Wellington's men stood firm and mowed them down in heaps with their rapid musketry and their cannon firing point-blank.

Even so, Wellington's situation was weakening and Blücher still had not arrived. Had Napoleon not

hesitated so long before committing his veterans of
the Imperial Guard, the outcome might have been
very different. It was not until early evening that he
sent them in, personally leading them part of the
way. In disciplined but incautious formation, jogg-
ing steadily up a ridge to a measured drumbeat and
chants of *'Vive l'Empereur!'*, they reached within
some fifty yards of Wellington's waiting Guards,
who rose from concealment and stopped them with
volley after volley. The attackers hesitated, turned,
and fled, and the pursuing bayonets were not
far behind.

Although the brave Old Guard did its best to
cover the retreat, the arrival of Blücher's force com-
pleted the rout. Napoleon himself narrowly escaped
capture by Prussian hussars. Some of his own men
would not have been averse to catching up with him;
he had made a last attempt to rally his force by telling
it that the approaching Prussians were French reinforcements, and many a man had stood fast and died
believing it.

He fled back to France, riding alone, followed by
two carriages containing Bertrand and five others.
His personal treasury was gone, scattered far and
wide over the ground for anyone to pick up. His
travelling carriage had been abandoned on the
battlefield; when the Prussians captured it they
found in it the State costume he had taken with him
for his triumphal entry into Brussels - mantle, diamond coronet, and all. They found, too, a diamond
necklace Pauline had given him on Elba, and gold
and silver tableware.

The man who arrived at the Élysée Palace at 8 a.m.
on 21 June resembled a pauper, untidy, dirty,
battered, utterly worn out. 'I can do no more,' he
said. He was in agony from his old bladder com-
plaint, for which he took refuge in a hot bath. In
spite of the crowds who shouted *'Aux armes! Vive
l'Empereur!'* there was no more he could do, no more
anyone could do. He was given two alternatives, to
be deposed or to abdicate, and chose abdication
again. Louis XVIII was moving back towards his
hastily vacated throne. A proclamation had gone out
for the punishment of those who had joined in or

promoted the so-called Hundred Days. Napoleon had no choice but to take himself, as ordered, to the port of Rochefort, where two frigates would be waiting.

On the way he paused at Malmaison, where Josephine's roses were in full bloom and beauty. People came to say goodbye; Joseph, Lucien, Madame Mère, Hortense, Marie Walewska and her son. For the last time he was in the place which he, who was not attached to places, had always loved, the country home where he had been as happy as it was possible for him to be, and where Josephine and he had been together. 'How beautiful it is,' he said, and put off again and again the moment when he must leave it.

Joseph had advised him to take refuge in America, as he intended to do with his own family. But plans became confused, and failed. In the end Joseph escaped in a fishing boat and boarded an American schooner, the *Pike*. On 15 July Napoleon surrendered to Captain Frederick Maitland, R.N., of H.M.S. *Bellerophon*, who received him without honours. Maitland agreed to take him to England on condition that the English Government should decide his fate, and seems to have suggested that he should seek asylum there. Napoleon therefore wrote to the Prince Regent:

> Your Royal Highness: Exposed to the factions which divide my Country, and to the Enmity of the greatest Powers of Europe, I have terminated my political career; and I come, like Themistocles, to throw myself upon the hospitality of the British People. I place myself under the protection of their laws, which I claim from your Royal Highness, as the most powerful, the most constant, and the most generous of my enemies.

What the Prince Regent thought of this is not recorded. Captain Maitland's initially cold demeanour thawed during the voyage to England. Napoleon was allowed to dine off his own gold plate, the dinner devised by his personal maître d'hôtel. He played *vingt-et-un* with the ship's officers, they entertained him with a play (Colman's comedy *The*

Poor Gentleman); he ate plenty of 'strong solid food'
and communed amiably with Maitland.

At daybreak on 24 July *Bellerophon* was approaching Dartmouth. Napoleon rose at six and went on
the poop to survey the coast. 'What a beautiful country!' he exclaimed. 'It very much resembles Porto
Ferrajo at Elba.' About 8.00 a.m. they anchored at
Torbay, and as the news of his presence soon got
about the bay filled up with boats full of people. *The
Times* might growl that he ought to have been greeted with a gallows, but instead he was the biggest
tourist attraction the Devon coast had ever seen.
The trippers regarded him with frank curiosity,
rather than enmity.

His appearance is described by several observers,
all agreeing more or less: sallow-complexioned,
rather fat, dressed in green uniform with red facings,
white waistcoat and breeches, military boots and
spurs, wearing the Grand Cross of the Legion of
Honour. His every appearance on the quarterdeck
was greeted with breathless interest. It would seem
that at this time he was mentally preparing himself
for residence in England, which his amazing capacity for shifting his ground made perfectly acceptable
to him. Once he had been a Corsican passionately
hating France, then a Frenchman passionately hating England; now he thought he might well become
a sort of courtesy Englishman, deeply respected and
received at Court. 'He professes his intention (if he
is allowed to reside in England) to adopt the English
customs and manners, and declares that he will
never meddle with politics more.'

On 26 July *Bellerophon* was ordered to Plymouth
Sound, where she lay closely guarded by two frigates. The Sound quickly filled up with boats
crowded with sightseers, training spy-glasses on the
deck where they hoped to see that familiar figure
appear. An observer recorded:

> Upwards of one thousand boats were from morn-
> ing to night round the *Bellerophon*. The seamen...
> adopted a curious mode to give an account to the
> curious spectators in the boats of the movements
> of Napoleon. They wrote in chalk on a board,

which they exhibited, a short account of his differ-
ent occupations. 'At breakfast'. 'In the cabin with
Captain Maitland'. 'Writing with his officers'.
'Going to dinner'. 'Coming upon deck' etc.

The sightseers often removed their hats, saluted and
cheered. The perhaps puzzled Emperor may have
noticed that John Bull was something of a sportsman.

His destination was officially announced to him
on 31 July: he was to go to St Helena, an island in the
South Atlantic, 1,200 miles off Portuguese West
Africa. It was not convenient for escaping to France,
or indeed for anything else. 'Its climate is healthy,'
said Lord Keith's communiqué smugly, 'and its
local position will allow of his being treated with
more indulgence than could be admitted in any
other spot, owing to the indispensable precautions
which it would be necessary to employ for the security of his person.'

Napoleon was not pleased. He objected to the
'violence exercised against his person'. He was the
guest of England and not its prisoner; he came of his
own accord to place himself under the protection of
its laws; the most sacred rights of hospitality were
violated in his person; he would never submit volun-
tarily to the outrage they were preparing for him,
and so on. It was useless. The episode of Elba had
discredited him in British eyes. On 4 August orders
came to *Bellerophon* to weigh and join the *Northum-
berland*, which was to take him to St Helena.

The strain had gone from Europe. 'The impress-
ment of seamen is directed to be discontinued at all
the seaports, as also the receiving of volunteers, except for the peace establishment. Orders have been
issued at the different ports to pay off the Navy; and
the seamen are to be sent to their respective homes,
in small vessels, to be in readiness for that purpose.'
The Napoleonic Wars were over.

St Helena was sighted on 17 October 1815, 'the
ugliest and most dismal rock conceivable... rising
like an enormous black wart from the face of the
deep.' The voyage had taken sixty-nine days.

Saint Helena

1815 – 1821

NAPOLEON'S EXILE was under the best conditions that could be afforded him. A London newspaper reported:

> By command of the Prince Regent, Lord Bathurst issued orders... to provide everything which would contribute to the domestic gratification and comfort of Napoleon Bonaparte in his new residence at St Helena. This order comprises every species of furniture, linen, glass ware, clothes, music, and musical instruments, which Bonaparte and the whole of his suite can possibly want for a period of more than three years. The directions for it were given in the most ample and unrestricted sense - no price in the first instance fixed, no particular quality of articles specified: the whole were to be made up in a style of pure and simple elegance, with this only reservation - that in no instance should any ornament or initial creep into the decorations which would be likely to recall to the mind of Bonaparte the former emblematical appendages of his imperial rank.

His suite consisted of twenty-six people, with Barry O'Meara, one of *Bellerophon*'s surgeons accompanying him as personal physician. Arrived at the small remote island, there was nothing for them but to settle down quickly. Napoleon's quarters were to be Longwood House, home of the Lieutenant-Governor, Colonel John Skelton. It was a modest, very English-looking house standing in its own grounds, needing improvements which would take time. Meanwhile, Napoleon expressed a wish to live at the guest house of a large cottage called The Briars, a name typical of the English suburban ambience that he would now be living in. It was the home of William Balcombe, naval agent and purveyor to the East India Company. Its setting was romantically rural, 'surrounded by barren mountains, it looked a perfect little paradise - an Eden blooming in the midst of desolation,' wrote Betsy Balcombe, the fourteen-year-old girl with whom the famous exile astonishingly made friends. She was lively, fearless, outspoken, not at all the sort of submissive female Napoleon had always approved of; but at this time in his life she was just the sort of company a lonely man needed. At first she was a little afraid of one with such a legend attached to him. Then, rapidly, she was won over.

> He seated himself on one of our cottage chairs, and after scanning our little apartment with his eagle glance, he complimented mamma on the pretty situation of The Briars. When once he began to speak, his fascinating smile and kind manner removed every vestige of the fear with which I had hitherto regarded him... His smile, and the expression of his eyes, could not be transmitted to canvas, and these constituted Napoleon's chief charm.

He enjoyed her tomboyish high spirits; she found in him an adult who laughed at her pranks instead of scolding her. They played jokes on each other which horrified Napoleon's retinue, whose behaviour towards him was governed by the strictest protocol. He corrected her French translations, he teased her by pretending to be a ghost; she went so far in her lèse-majesté that her stern father imprisoned her in a rat-ridden cellar every day for a week, while Napoleon cheered her up with jokes and consolation through the bars of the window.

> I never met with any one who bore childish liberties

so well as Napoleon. He seemed to enter into every
sort of mirth or fun with the glee of a child, and
though I have often tried his patience severely, I
never knew him lose his temper or fall back upon
his rank or age...

After two months of this happy companionship
Napoleon was summoned to Longwood, now ready
for him. Betsy wept bitterly. 'You must not cry,
Mademoiselle Betsee, you must come and see me
next week, and very often.' She did, and was always
welcome, though she found him 'more subject to
depression of spirits than when at the Briars'. Of all
the accounts and descriptions of Napoleon, Betsy
Balcombe's is surely the most unusual, and by far
the most attractive. Perhaps he could only be truly
charming and natural once the power he had wield-
ed was taken out of his hands.

Life at Longwood was not stimulating to one who
had been supremely a man of action. It was a sprawl-
ing house of which he had two rooms out of the
twenty-three. His officers were mostly lodged at the
other end of the house, servants in the attics. It was a
damp house and, like The Briars, infested with rats.
From the garden the view was not inspiring: a bare,
wind-tortured landscape, volcanic mountains behind, and the camp at Deadwood, where the red
coats of sentries reminded him that he was a captive.
Should he venture to break bounds, semaphore sig-
nals would go up. Almost three thousand soldiers
were his jailers.

Within limits, he could go riding unescorted.
Sometimes he would drive, with some of his staff
and any visitors, in a six-horse carriage through
rough country, along bad roads. When it rained,
and it often did, he could read or dictate his
Memoirs to Count Las Cases. Then there was the
ceremony of the bath, a ritual still immensely important to Napoleon. In the evening there was card-
playing, and a formal dinner, exactly as if they were
all back at the Tuileries; then bed, and so on, day
after day.

After a year of it, an irritant arrived to disturb the
calm of Longwood. It came in the form of the new

English governor, Sir Hudson Lowe. He brought orders from London that the annual expenditure of the household must be reduced from £12,000 to £8,000. Lowe's portrait shows a long-nosed, tight-lipped face with bad-tempered eyes under bushy brows, and arms aggressively folded; he might be a headmaster arraigning a naughty schoolboy, which was, roughly, his attitude. He antagonised Napoleon from the first by sending up his compliments to 'General Bonaparte', who was then in bed. Napoleon replied that he was not a general, and remained in bed. The Duke of Wellington, who had once called Lowe a damned fool, thought him a very bad choice for the St Helena post. Suspicious, jealous, petty-minded, Lowe antagonised not only Napoleon but his entire staff, tightening regulations, limiting Napoleon's exercise area, reviving early directives which had been allowed to lapse, such as the one that an English officer must see Napoleon at least twice a day. He had his own skin to think of, and he was not going to have a repetition of Elba. 'He looked very much like a person who would not let his prisoner escape if he could help it,' someone said.

Because of Lowe's restrictions, visitors became fewer, and there were therefore fewer of the opportunities Napoleon must have longed for - to get messages to sympathisers, somehow to contrive an escape or at worst a change of prison from that dreary, remote island. Soon he and Lowe had ceased to meet - after one fearful explosion of temper Napoleon refused to admit him again - but the battle between them went on. A crisis came in 1816 when Lowe had Las Cases and his young son arrested on a charge of 'clandestine correspondence'. It was true; Las Cases's servant had been smuggling letters out for delivery in England to various parties, written on white satin and sewn into the lining of a coat. The Memoirs Las Cases had taken down from Napoleon's dictation were all in Lowe's possession. Las Cases and his son were deported, the first of Napoleon's friends to leave St Helena.

Next to go were the Balcombes, in March 1818. Betsy had even more reason to weep now than when Napoleon had left The Briars. She cried so much that he had to provide her with a handkerchief, which he then gave her to keep as a memento. Lowe had not approved of the family's friendship with Napoleon. Then the second of his suite, General Gourgaud, left. He had quarrelled violently with other exiles, General Montholon and his family. The next loss was by death: Cipriani, Napoleon's steward and confidant, who could be trusted with letters, messages, transactions of all sorts to the prisoner's advantage, was taken ill during dinner one night and died four days later.

Napoleon's own health had begun deteriorating in 1817. Mysterious pains, poor appetite, recurring symptoms of lassitude and sleeplessness, troubled him. His doctor, O'Meara, claimed that there was some form of hepatitis which was connected with the climate of St Helena. A new physician, Dr Antommarchi, was sent out, arriving on 18 September 1819. By this time Napoleon was more alone than ever. Madame Montholon, who may or may not have been his mistress, had gone home, taking her three children; whatever their relationship, she had at least been lively feminine society. Only Count Montholon remained, and Count and Countess Bertrand, and Napoleon's valet, the devoted Louis Marchand. Napoleon's life was lonely, monotonous and dreary. It was not to last much longer.

Late in 1820 Montholon wrote to his wife that Napoleon was suffering from a *'maladie de langueur'*. He had other painful and distressing symptoms which Antommarchi diagnosed as chronic hepatitis. He tried to help himself by attempting out-of-door exercise, forcing himself to eat, and begging the doctor to give him hope rather than medicines. On 17 March 1821 he took his last carriage-ride, then retired to his bed.

Knowing himself at death's door, he began to draw up his will, first by his own hand and then dictating it. He wished to be buried in Paris, in Père Lachaise; all his personal possessions were left to his son, now known as the Duke of Reichstadt: the sword of Austerlitz, the blue cloak of Marengo, Sobieski's sabre, the great chain of the Légion d'Honneur, 'Henry IV hat and my plume', relics of past glories. The humbler items make a pathetic list: 'The little gilt clock now in my bedroom... my three silver brandy flasks, which my grooms carried into the field... my two watches, and the chain made of the Empress's hair... 1 little box full of my snuff.' There were legacies of money and specific gifts to relatives and friends - Montholon, Bertrand, Marchand, old comrades in arms and their children; he thought of everybody. Well for him that he did not know his cherished possessions would never reach his son.

On 5 May 1821, after a day of unconsciousness, surrounded by the quiet company of friends and servants, Napoleon died. The last words he was heard to speak before lapsing into a coma were *'France... mon fils... armée.'* Before that he had said 'Josephine'.

They buried him in Slane's Valley, about two miles from Longwood, under willow-trees. The inscription on the outer coffin should have read 'Napoleon', followed by the dates of his birth and death, but Lowe's meanness and spite followed him literally to the grave, insisting that the name should be 'Napoleon Bonaparte' or nothing. It was nothing. The grave remained anonymous until the October day in 1840 when men came to exhume the body, and take it home to France. There it lies still, in the crypt of l'Église Royale, in the Hôtel des Invalides, France's most revered secular shrine.

The dynasty Napoleon had tried so desperately to found came to nothing, as is the way of non-royal dynasties. Marie Louise soon lost interest in her son, having other preoccupations in her morganatic second husband, Count Adam Albert von Neipperg, and their two children; she later married a Baron Werklein. The child who had been King of Rome and retitled Duke of Reichstadt was brought up as an Austrian prince, kept away from everything to do with France or his father. When the possessions Napoleon had willed to him arrived, the bearers were ordered to deliver them to the Austrian Embassy in Paris, where they would be given a signed receipt. The young Duke never saw them. After his death from tuberculosis in 1832 they passed to his grandmother, Madame Mère, who did not die until 1836, having outlived both Napoleon and his son.

Hortense's son Louis-Napoleon became the head of the Bonaparte clan on the death of his cousin, and in 1852, although he had pledged himself to serve under the flag of the Republic, became Napoleon III, ruler of the Second Empire. His only son, the Prince Imperial, was killed in the Zulu campaign of 1879. So ended the rule, and the hopes, of the Bonapartes.

Napoleon

1769 – 1821

Letizia (1750-1836).

Carlo-Maria Buonaparte
(1746-1785).

Napoleon's parents. Thirteen children were born but only five
boys and three girls survived.

Directing mock battles in the snow at the Military School in Brienne, where Napoleon was to remain until October 1784.

The *École Militaire* in Paris. Napoleon passed out in September 1785, receiving his commission with the rank of 2nd lieutenant.

The house in Ajaccio, Corsica, where Napoleon was born on 15 August 1769.

The storming of the Bastille, 14 July 1789.

The Death of Marat, July 1793.

'To Versailles! To Versailles!' The hungry mob march on Versailles for bread.

The execution of Louis XVI on 21 January 1793.

Beginning in 1789, the French Revolution was a time of immense upheaval as the 'Old Régime' broke down in the midst of national disorder and violence culminating in the 'Reign of Terror' in 1793-1794.

Napoleon working the gun at Toulon in December 1793. A contemporary British cartoon depicting Napoleon's first major battle, which led to immediate promotion.

Josephine de Beauharnais (1763-1814), after her separation from her first husband.

Alexandre, Vicomte de Beauharnais (1760-1794). Shortly after their separation he was arrested as a traitor to the Revolution and guillotined.

Two days after his marriage to Josephine in March 1796, Napoleon left her to take up his new post as General-in-Chief of the French Army of Italy. This engraving shows the legendary charge at Arcola.

The Battle of Rivoli (January 1787). His success in Italy brought him great honour and acclaim on his triumphant return to France.

Napoleon leaving Toulon in 1798 with an army of 30,000 men. The Army of the Orient landed in Egypt in July.

A medal depicting Napoleon
addressing his troops before the
Battle of the Pyramids (July 1798).

The Battle of Aboukir (July 1799). A crushing defeat for the Turks. Shortly after this victory Napoleon sailed for home, landing in France in October to a hero's welcome.

FLIGHT FROM EGYPT.

Napoleon's departure from Egypt seen through the eyes of a British satirist in this cartoon showing him secretly slipping away while his army slept.

Napoleon was elected First Consul on 19 February 1800.

Originally sharing the position with Cambacères and Le Brun, Napoleon was later appointed First Consul for life in 1802.

Josephine, the well known portrait by Gerard.

La Malmaison, near Versailles, the country home of the First Consul and the First Lady of the land.

Josephine drawing a portrait from a bust of the First Consul.

Crossing the Alps in May 1800. Leading his troops in the example of Hannibal, Napoleon intended to crush the Austrians in a surprise attack.

The Battle of Marengo (June 1800).

An assassination attempt on Napoleon in October 1800.

The impending war with England led to fantastic projects to cross the Channel as in this contemporary engraving of balloons, barges, tunnels, and men leaping from large kites.

Typical British cartoons of the resumption of war with France in May 1803.

The Coronation of Napoleon and Josephine as Emperor and Empress.
The ceremony took place on 2 December 1804.

The Battle of Trafalgar (October 1805). Nelson destroyed the Franco-Spanish fleet without loss of a single ship, though at the cost of his own life.
Inset: Lord Nelson (1758-1805).

The eve of the Battle of Austerlitz (December 1805). Napoleon visits the village where the troops are bivouacked.

Louis Bonaparte (1778-1846). Napoleon's brother who became King of Holland in 1806 but abdicated four years later.

Field Marshal Gebhard von Blücher (1742-1819). He suffered a heavy defeat for the Prussians at Jena, but was to be avenged in the Battle of Waterloo, nine years later.

Napoleon reviewing the troops at the Battle of Jena (October 1806).

Jerome Bonaparte (1784-1860). Napoleon's youngest brother who was named King of Westphalia in 1807.

Joseph Bonaparte (1768-1844). Napoleon's elder brother who was made King of Naples in 1806 and King of Spain in 1808.

Napoleon receiving the keys to the city of Berlin in October 1806.

Lucien Bonaparte (1775-1840). Napoleon's brother who became Prince of Canino in 1814.

The Battle of Eylau (February 1807).

Countess Marie Walewska. Napoleon met and fell in love with her in January 1807. She was later to have an illegitimate son by him.